Peter Giles

# A Basic Countertenor Method
# for teacher and student

Foreword by Barry Rose

Kahn & Averill
London

Published by Kahn & Averill
2-10 Plantation Road
Amersham, Buckinghamshire, HP6 6HJ
United Kingdom

www.kahnandaverill.co.uk

First published in Great Britain in 1987 by Thames Publishing

This revised edition published in 2005 by Kahn & Averill



Back cover illustration by Peter Giles
Cover design by Simon Stern

Printed in Great Britain by Halstan UK
2-10 Plantation Road
Amersham, Buckinghamshire, HP6 6HJ
United Kingdom

www.halstan.co.uk



ISBN 978-1-871-08282-1

# Contents

# Foreword to the 1987 edition

There is no sound anywhere in the world to compare with a well-trained choir of men and boys. For centuries, the stones of our cathedrals and collegiate chapels have resounded to choral music – that daily offering which strives to match the perfection of wood and stone carvings, the beauty of the stained-glass windows and the inspired architecture of so many of our great ecclesiastical buildings.

Worship must always be the best that we can offer, and choirs have always had their special part to play – the pure yet vibrant quality of the treble voices, the telling sonority of the tenors and basses, and, above all, the unique and distinctive timbre of the counter-tenor. Though a voice both sacred and secular, as Peter Giles explains, it was thanks to the medieval church that the counter-tenor 'came originally into formal and valued use, flourished, survived neglect in the secular world and re-emerged to take its rightful place in the world once more'.

I first heard the counter-tenor voice on some old and not very distinguished recordings of cathedral choirs, made in the 1930s. Not only was the recording poor, but often so was the alto sound – frequently hooty, wobbly and seemingly lacking in technique, though there must have been exceptions amongst singers. However, they were little in evidence. No wonder, in those years of my youth, that I used to mis-spell the word as OWLTO! So perhaps a renaissance was due. A renaissance is just what happened in Canterbury, in the dark days of World War II, when a new alto lay-clerk was appointed to the cathedral choir. His name was Alfred Deller; and I would suggest that every counter-tenor since then owes something of his sounds and ability to the example of this one man, whose voice first reached many listeners outside Canterbury through the BBC Third Programme, and that first HMV record of Purcell's 'Music for a While'.

Alfred Deller's art lives, not only in his recordings but is passed on by singer-teachers, who themselves fashioned their sound on what they heard when they first started to sing the alto line. Today's counter-tenors travel the world, they broadcast, they record constantly. We can sit in concert hall, cathedral, and in our homes, hear the exquisite sound, admire the vocal expertise and, now, considerable technique.

But how is it done? Drawn from his 27 years' experience as a cathedral lay-clerk and solo singer, Peter Giles gives us a comprehensive guide, from the making of the first sounds to acquiring the complete technique. The vital aspects of resonance, differing registers, breathing, vocal agility, are all carefully explained; not just in words but also with specially drawn diagrams by the author himself. There are graded vocal exercises to encourage us to produce the sounds, which have been so carefully and clearly explained. This is, in fact, the complete manual for the teacher and the would-be counter-tenor, and is appropriately written – by a counter-tenor.

Barry Rose
May, 1987

*Master of the Choirs, The King's School, Canterbury*
*Music Adviser to the Head of Religious Broadcasting, BBC*

# Preface and introduction

This Preface, while being essentially that of the first edition, has undergone some important adjustment. The same is true of the work as a whole, in that this new edition has offered valuable opportunities for re-examination of the text throughout; though of course, Dr Barry Rose's Foreword has been left exactly as he wrote it.

During investigation of the first edition, sixteen years after its publication, I discovered little for which I have anxiously awaited the opportunity to alter; but inevitably, besides some subtle updating, some phraseology was found to be in need of adjustment or change. Likewise, certain areas needed clarification, and a few typographical errors and oddities required correction.

People who devise instrumental or vocal methods could be:

1 The distinguished international solo artist.
2 The well-known (or less well-known) professional soloist.
3 The experienced general professional whose agenda and routine involves solo work regularly.
4 The experienced general professional.
5 The highly competent, perhaps celebrated, professional teacher.

The *raison d'être* of those in category 5 is obvious; but it could be assumed that those in categories 1–4 write with at least some (often a great deal of) experience of teaching and developing technique in others. Certainly, when devising a practical course (as in any form of pedagogy), it appears essential to have a hunger to share enthusiasm, research, and first-hand knowledge and experience.

In common with all singing methods, this one has the obvious purpose of helping the student towards a strong and versatile vocal technique, which will remain in good order for many years. No doubt there are differences of opinion on what is, or is not, basic technique, but the essential foundations of the following method have withstood the test of time. I owe much to my vocal training with John Whitworth, who, after Alfred Deller, was probably the most influential singer during and immediately following the revival of secular solo countertenor singing in the 1940s and 50s.

John Whitworth taught me from 1961 to 1966. His own vocal training had been excellently grounded. He studied under the tenor Frank Titterton, and later with Robert Poole. I mention this because it is important to underline the essential pedigree of my teaching method: firmly-based mainstream, mixed with the transforming impact of White's Technique. During the nineteen-eighties, I worked with Arthur D Hewlett, whose valuable help and teaching expertise, grounded in the theories and practice of his teacher and mentor, Ernest George White (1863–1940), widened and enriched my singing and pedagogy.

Most creative artists find the need to review their technique at intervals. Sometimes, the work of singers begins to suffer from a variety of regime or *diktat*. A prime example in England, to which the countertenor can fall victim (because he tends to be working in such vocal ensembles for at least part of his professional life) is that of the busy professional cathedral choir. It requires daily commitment. It also demands an unusually wide vocal range and stylistic adjustment, sometimes at short notice, which might not feel welcome at that particular point, but which nevertheless has to be dealt with successfully. Diversity can be healthful and exciting when it is a matter of personal choice; but in ensemble – and English cathedral choirs and their Organists and Masters of the Choristers are absolutely no exception – compulsory vocal diversity is always the result of decisions made by the musical director. It must be said, of course, that the professional choir, or any expert ensemble, has strict requirements of balance, blend and tonal adjustment. This is as it should be.

Some years ago, these factors began to affect my own solo and trio work. I felt a need to review my approach. In so doing, I found it necessary to re-formulate and focus my technique and *raison d'être* – to ask myself questions and demand answers. I emerged from this process strengthened and regenerated, ready for the next stage of my vocal and aesthetic development. This renewed positive awareness was greatly assisted by my fortunate introduction to White's Technique and to the theories behind it, which proved invaluable and vocal-life renewing. They have continued to be so.

My long and varied experiences in both practice and research seem a dependable platform from which to write this work. Over my years as a countertenor, I have examined (and usually found unsatisfactory) many general vocal treatises available. While there are satisfactory teachers of countertenors; few, so far, seem to write treatises of any type.

So far as general teachers are concerned, I have long been struck by the written and oral admission of many of these that they know nothing of countertenors. Because of this, many refuse to take the male high voice on at all, or they try to persuade the aspiring countertenor to transfer to another vocal-range. Others, despite their admitted lack of familiarity with this vocal type, nevertheless accept countertenors as pupils, usually with mixed results. As one would expect, they usually teach basic singing principles and technique perfectly well; but not surprisingly, essential historical countertenor method is totally absent.

Thankfully, matters have improved somewhat since the first edition of this work appeared, in that more countertenors are themselves teaching countertenors. Yet there are not enough to go round; and in any case, one sometimes suspects that countertenors who teach others, though they might be excellent singers, do not themselves always seem to know enough about teaching their subject, or the depth of relevant historical knowledge required.

From this overall general situation has come a method prepared especially to assist the *teacher* of the male high voice, and for the needs of this vocal-range. I would stress, however, that this work is certainly not designed to set the countertenor apart, but to suggest that other vocal ranges – notably the lyric and 'early music' tenor – could benefit from the historically-aware approach it employs.

In addition to its main purpose as a tool for teachers, it is intended to be useful as a refresher or alternative approach for existing singers. It is also designed to assist a student forced to work alone. This should be very much a second option. Teaching yourself is a last resort, and is recommended reluctantly only when unusual circumstances dictate it.

The present course may therefore be used at several different levels and from varied directions. It must be emphasized that, however well-ordered and planned, *no practical course, especially a written, technical method, can turn anyone into an artist. In addition to vocal development, study of musicianship and interpretation must be made, and experience gained, in order that the student acquires skill and sensitivity as a creative performer. (Anything more, the achievement of true artist status, is a gift given only to a few, its existence, hopefully, to be recognised by others.)* The teacher will of course know all this perfectly well, but the lone student is advised to ensure that the extra-vocal essentials, inevitably absent from a work of this sort, are covered elsewhere.

It is for this reason, for example, that I recommend the Vaccai course, which, despite its title, is essentially for vocal musicianship, not voice production. (See page 77 and the Booklist.) Ideally, my comprehensive book, *The History and Technique of the Counter- Tenor* (Scolar Press / Ashgate, 1994), should be read as an essential companion to this present Method. In addition, *Les Contre-ténors: Mythes & Réalités*, my passerelle for the recording company Harmonia Mundi (1999), which includes two CDs of important countertenors, should be sought out.

Surprise may be registered at my inclusion of some exercises by Sims Reeves (1818–1900), the celebrated Victorian tenor, in view of his known opinion of the countertenor. It dates from the late 1830s. Presumably, because his initial vocal training was as a youthful countertenor, he only scorned the genre after encountering the impact of the 19th-century vocal 'revolution'. At any rate, suitably adapted, his exercises are excellent for our purpose, and some may have been those with which he was trained himself.

Study *Think Afresh About the Voice*, by Arthur D Hewlett. The unconventional theories of Ernest George White, which Hewlett expounds expertly and demonstrates thoroughly, are based on the method known originally as sinus tone production. Because this term seems to have caused confusion and misunderstanding amongst more conventional vocal pedagogues, quite unnecessarily, and still can; the method tends today to be known as White's Technique.

I make no apologies for recommending the work of student, not master, initially at least; for Hewlett slightly tempers some of White's more difficult ideas, and is willing to compromise in certain areas of argument.

White's theories may sometimes *appear* long discounted, particularly by the ultra-conservative wing of the orthodox teaching world, but do not be deceived. There seems in the world of vocal pedagogy a stirring, an enquiring, which involves, directly or indirectly, a quite discernible move towards re-examining ideas with which White was first associated. There is no doubt, of course, that his practical method works, and works very well.

As Hewlett says on page 80 of his book: 'Sinus tone has been found to bear fruit with voices of any calibre; enriching the talented; building up the fair to moderate; and, when necessary, repairing the damaged or creating the non-existent.' What more could be asked of any method – except that it be assimilated properly and used well? Sometimes, the benefits of this method only take hold late in the day. For example, White's thesis and Hewlett's expansion of it won the tenors Sir Peter Pears* and Wilfred Brown over towards the end of their lives.

In *Organists' Review* for October 1971 there was an article by Charles Cleall, one of HM Inspectors of Schools, a music specialist, whose own research on the range and compass of voices is of great significance. In it, he declares: 'The remedial work of sinus-tone teachers is enough to give us reason to attend to their methods; and the evenness and freedom from strain of their pupils is quite enviable. Few teachers of singing have done so much good and so little damage (indeed, it might be provable that they have never damaged a voice). They describe concepts that lead to maximum control and healthy practice.'

I include all that for good reason. I suspect that White's methods, formulated in the early twentieth century, might have something in common with almost lost classical or *bel canto* practices of vocal placement, handed down by verbal instruction and practical demonstration until the mid-nineteenth. These classical practices had been used and taught by all-important singers, it would seem, including the most outstanding of all time – the castrati. Even Manuel Del Popolo Vicente Garcia (1775–1832) – distinguished tenor and teacher; father of the Manuel Garcia whose laryngoscope laid down the basis for conventional modern teaching methods – is thought to have been trained for a while by Giuseppe Aprile (1738–1814), a castrato. Aprile's vocal method and teaching were of the classical school, inevitably; as, presumably, were Garcia the elder's. The younger Garcia (1805–1906) began study under his father, yet eventually the admittedly valuable but often inhibiting nature of his own work was to undermine many of the insights of classical methods. White's work in England, in the first decades of the twentieth century, seems to have helped redress the balance, although it

---

* See Pears's Foreword to Hewlett's *Think Afresh About the Voice* (1973).

was greeted with hostility by the establishment of the time in this country, and total disregard by many teachers in the years since.

Of course, Garcia's laryngoscope had not changed everything in an instant. The old teaching methods died slowly in certain sheltered or conservative spheres. For example, the celebrated operatic *diva*, Madame Emma Calvé (1858–1942), was taught a technique for high voice by one of the last castrati of the Sistine Chapel, Domenico Mustapha (1829–1912), which involved practising for three years with the mouth closed. I mention this now because study of White's Technique begins with the hum, and, apparently like Calvé's work with Mustapha, is technique taught with minimum theory but maximum patient encouragement of sensation, and inculcation of mental image. Today, White's Technique could be regarded as cousin to the well-known Alexander Technique, used by many in recent years as a beneficial approach to physical and mental well-being.

I should underline that purely laryngeal aspects of the vocal function are best not dwelt on in detail by the student, particularly when working without a teacher, and in any case not till much later in the present course. This is the reason why most of the laryngeal matter and discussion is placed at the end of the book. Some would argue that it should not be discussed at all – especially in a work which might be in the hands of an unsupervised student, when laryngeal fixation and imagery could open up dangers of vocal inhibition.

Nevertheless, it is necessary for the teacher to be fully aware of how laryngeal considerations affect the countertenor.

Because pre-Garcia singing teachers of the classical school taught effectively without the benefits, or otherwise, of the detailed anatomical knowledge available now, it seems a good plan, particularly in that the countertenor is first and foremost an historical voice, to concentrate, to begin with, on sensation, placing and *resonance*, as pre-Garcia teachers surely must have done; not with the intricate workings of the larynx. Clearly, it is important never to seek or allow consciousness of the larynx, particularly *whilst performing*; just as the athlete does not normally think about the structure and workings of his body while actually competing. Connected with this, all mention throughout this manual of specific registers should be regarded as useful if crude points of reference, not as continual reminders of the workings of the vocal folds.

In the text throughout this course, I refer to the pitch of notes according to the more straightforward American system, which seems clearer than that of Helmholz, though I show his scheme directly below mine:

I should also say that certain areas of technical study have been touched on only lightly, or even omitted. The practical development of vibrato, for example, occupies the first category. It is, of course, properly a strictly controlled, ornamental effect, used at will. Excellent theoreticians and teachers have gone into it in detail and into more important matters (such as breathing technique, and the forming and singing of Italian and English vowels).

I have therefore provided relatively brief discussion of vowels, breathing and vibrato. Most teachers will not need my input on these. Students working alone may well wish to consult Julian Gardiner's *A Guide to Good Singing and Speech*, Charles Kennedy Scott's *The Fundamentals of Singing*, and my own *The History and Technique of the Counter-Tenor* on these particular matters, but definitely not till well into the present course, and before Sections D and E.

It is seldom that a student of any voice-range is not already singing elsewhere, probably in choir or ensemble. The eternal problem is ensuring that good work done during lessons and specific personal practice is not undone almost immediately by choral demands by unthinking musical directors. If possible, therefore, the student should suspend outside vocal involvement whilst undergoing the present course.

Temporary suspension of any public performance may well be relatively easy for the man working to be a full-time soloist. On the other hand, it would be impossible for young cathedral lay-clerks, or those who are required to sing daily in comparable professional positions, who wish to use this course for renewal or refinement –  with or without a teacher. While care must be taken by all students to adjust their vocal technique gently, as they go; those who find themselves unable to suspend public performance must try to rehearse privately the music they are required to sing, using this opportunity to apply their new techniques. In time, with patience, they will find that they can employ them unselfconsciously in performance.

Loud singing must be avoided, as ideally should solos (however modest they seem) until new techniques are well established. The student should seek ways of using musical material met as additional exercises – and be careful what music he meets! Choir or ensemble singers should explain their temporary position to the choir director. Willingness to compromise is essential. There are various positive, perfectly acceptable ways of dealing with the situation. For the student in ensemble, whenever possible, it is important to avoid or 'ghost' if confronted with passages for which he does not yet feel prepared.

There are many opposing views on all aspects of vocal pedagogy and training. It is plainly impossible to advocate and champion techniques and practices acceptable to all schools and traditions of thought. Teachers and students are asked to bear in mind throughout that I have endeavoured to bring together two main approaches previously, but wrongly, considered fundamentally incompatible. Inevitably, there will be people who find it difficult to come to terms with this; but this course may convince them that such a marriage is not unreasonable.

I have therefore striven to adopt a positive, direct, if personal, approach, based on English tradition and tonal ideals initially (but emphatically without the stretched-down, distended-jaw approach), together with the use of what are surely essential vocal criteria which have proved themselves valuable in other European traditions. We must always remember that the countertenor voice-range was used widely in different centuries, in countries with different vocal traditions. We should be conscious also that much historical evidence exists for known singers working in countries other than their own. Therefore, as in any art form, cross-fertilization was likely.

*Because I hope to be addressing the teacher, I employ the language of one singer to another. Because I must also allow for the absence of a teacher, I try to phrase for the student, too.* I hope that the balance is successful. Particularly in the main areas of practical instruction, my phraseology is not that of a laryngologist, or academic.* I use more detailed technical terms and explanation for obvious reasons in Section D: even

---

* There are no detailed references in the text which follows because this is primarily a practical manual.

today, the countertenor sometimes needs to explain and justify voice, technique, and even his existence, usually to the conservative of mind; but my aim, and approach, over-all, is based essentially on *mental image*. The course should normally be used in exact order as printed; though, at the discretion of the teacher, certain exercises might be thought better displaced slightly, to suit the needs of the individual student. When practising, remember the old adage 'little and often'.

As we approach the beginning of this work, I suggest that, if forced to work unsupervised, the beginner-student may wish to start with the Method itself (i.e. Section B), returning later to Section A, the content of which is placed early in the book for the convenience and use of teachers and more experienced students. A suitable point at which to return might be page 41; though pages 6–9 and 13–17 should perhaps be studied earlier.

It will be noticed that in this new edition I have adopted the single, un-hyphenated form of the title 'countertenor'. While the hyphenated version is as historically accurate, the former is less fussy.

Finally, I must deal with the inevitable question asked by most students at the start of most courses, of all varieties: 'How long will it take?' The answer appropriate to a vocal course is, simply, 'As long as it *does* take,' because each student is quite different. Some find this open-ended concept difficult to accept, and they become impatient. Some learn patience; a few do not, and go sadly away. *The hard truth is that, little which is ultimately worthwhile can be rushed. It is a hard lesson for today's obsession with instant result.*

I hope that the student will not turn away, sadly or otherwise, but persevere with a disciplined, unrushed approach; never allowing himself to proceed until each exercise is mastered in depth. If it is any consolation, he might reflect that, however long the course takes to complete satisfactorily, it can never equal the years it has taken the author to experience first-hand; to research, to order, set out, and finally to present this basic countertenor method.

Peter Giles 1986
*(revised 2004)*

# Acknowledgements

Though the author is alone responsible for the matter contained in the original work, producing such a book required the expert advice of several people. I thank John Whitworth, Charles Cleall, Arthur D Hewlett, Grayston Burgess, the late Frederic Hodgson, and Alan Arduoin, FRCS, DLO, for reading the original manuscript, and for their valuable help and suggestions. I thank my own students, too, past and present, for their useful if mostly inadvertent contributions!

For a contribution even more obvious, I thank Dr Barry Rose for his valuable Foreword. Here may I thank Jane Farrell for editing and proofreading and Simon Stern for help over and above his design brief.

# Historical note

Though, inevitably, the text deals with certain matters *en route*, in this essentially practical manual there is little point in attempting to cover much formal historical ground, especially as I have written at length on this in *The History and Technique of the Counter-Tenor*. However, all students should have a basic historical outline of their instrument immediately at hand.

There has been, and still is, much argument over the countertenor voice. I have long come to the conclusion that it is not so much a single voice as a small family type, the members of which are all perfectly legitimate, and which I shall later describe.

The countertenor, or alto (male, of course) is an inseparable part of most early music. Its origins are ancient: 'falsetto'-based register has been used since the beginnings of the human race. The contratenor part, from which the countertenor title came, was an integral ingredient in the development of European harmony and counter-point. The voice range or ranges that sprang from this part enjoyed a growth, popularity and repertoire considerable and predictable.

After all, for centuries, women's voices were not normally employed, it seems, on state or comparable ceremonial and official court occasions; or in church (except in convents); or, seemingly, on formal musical occasions; or in most drama. On the other hand, men and women would surely have sung together on occasion in the domestic or essentially informal *milieu*, at most levels of society, in all periods. But even into the nineteenth century the male high voice was available there too, and indeed seems to have survived throughout the century and beyond in family gatherings, in peripheral manner at any rate.

At those medieval, but essentially timeless, roistering gatherings – concerned, for example, with inebriation, celebration, hay-making, merry-making, and very uncourtly love – the higher male voices probably would have been used often for parody, and to comic effect. The woman's part of 'conversation' songs or dialogues, as revealed in surviving medieval and later manuscripts, thus could have been sung by either women or men. No doubt, role-reversal was constant, in humorous *genre* at least; for informal areas of medieval life seem to have involved something of a free-for-all: a facet of human life which has never been entirely absent, and is certainly with us today.

Thus it seems undeniable that in order to perform most surviving early music authentically, formal and informal, over the vocal ranges in question here, the availability and timbres of the countertenor in one or other of his varieties is essential. In addition to early music a growing modern repertoire has developed since the revival of the secular solo countertenor forty years ago. This, however, sometimes shows a tendency towards a rather higher overall tessitura than in earlier centuries.

During an almost total absence of just over one hundred years from the 'serious' concert platform (although it was used from time to time for the light-ballad genre), this male voice-range survived almost uniquely, and not always merely in modest or humble manner, in English cathedral and similar choirs, and glee clubs. Most of its earlier solo and ensemble repertoire has either had to be rescued from other voices or re-discovered by research. Although it cannot compete with the sheer brilliance, power and impact of the best evirati; who were, and will probably forever be, matchless vocally; the sound, and indeed often the bodily height, if rarely the physique of the powerfully developed high falsettist countertenor, is thought generally to evoke the castrato most nearly, and to be a convincing substitute. Stage presence is an essential aspect. So this vocal area opens up much additional repertoire to the countertenor of today, especially as castrati were sometimes deputized for, on stage and platform, by falsettists. It is especially fitting because, originally, castrati displaced falsetti. This is documented well with regard to the Sistine Chapel. I mention this to cite a well-known example, and one particular vocal arena – that of the church.

It is thanks largely to the church, directly and indirectly, that the countertenor voice came originally into important formal and valued use, flourished, survived neglect in the secular world, and re-emerged to take its rightful place in the world once more.

# The steady voice

The problems and much-debated subject of vibrato and tremolo have to be faced, perhaps sooner than later. Most certainly not a topic affecting only the countertenor, it impinges on all voice-ranges and types, especially in early-music performance.

As somebody once remarked, perceptively, it is easy to see the attraction of vibrato. The problems of poor intonation can almost disappear when the variation of pitch across and for each note is so obligingly wide. It is certainly true that the purer and straighter the note, the less can the singer get away with suspect intonation.

Vibrato and tremolo seem to have been confused by different theorists of different periods. What is nowadays called vibrato, but has been termed tremolo, properly controlled, should be thought of as an ornamental effect switched on and off at will. Used continuously, as by most modern singers, it can lose its charm and can rob the music of its freshness. This is especially a danger in performing early music. On the other hand, the deliciously cartouched artificiality of the Baroque demands its availability – not its absolutely continuous use – in solo singing at least. Of course, various early-music authorities have written on the subject with some disagreement. The student will find suggestions for study in the Booklist. It is true to say that continuous *voce bianca* – white, colourless voice – seems to be frowned on too. As a general guide, therefore, the student is advised to keep the vocal quality alive and pleasantly colourful without pitch wobble.

Here are a few thought-provoking quotations on tremolo/vibrato. We start with wise words of Pier Francesco Tosi, from his famous *Observations on the Florid Song* (1743, but originally published in Italy in 1723 as *Opinioni de' cantori antichi e moderni*). The modern edition* adds useful notes:

---

* Edited by Michael Pilkington (Stainer & Bell 1987), p 8.

> Let him learn to hold out the notes without a shrillness like a trumpet, or trembling; and if at the beginning [the master] made him hold out every note the length of two bars, the improvement would be the greater. Otherwise from the natural inclination that the beginner has to keep the voice in motion, and the trouble in holding it out, he will get a habit, and not be able to fix it, and will become subject to a fluttering in the manner of all those that sing in a very bad taste.

Michael Pilkington adds: 'By "fix it," Tosi means "hold (the long note) firmly in place," not "correct the error," a use of the expression introduced in the USA in the 19th century. This passage is a warning against excessive vibrato.'

Incidentally, Manuel Garcia's important treatise *Art of Singing* (1847) contains nothing about vibrato or tremolo, but plenty on steadiness of voice.

In 1889, *The Musical Times* commented on the first performance of Wagner's *Das Rheingold:*

> At last an occasion has been found for that vocal defect, the tremolo. The Rhine Maidens in New York are all 'wobblers' of a pronounced description, but they have a press friend who points out that, as they are supposed to be singing underwater, the effect of their performance is realistic. So true is it that nothing has been created in vain.*

As the 19th century ends, the great Victorian tenor, Sims Reeves, gives good counsel:

> It is scarcely necessary to describe the tremolo. Five out of every six modern singers are afflicted with it, and consequently there is a great deal of make-believe that the tremolo is a splendid vehicle for the expression of sentiment and passion. But experience soon proves that an audience never mistakes affectation – and tremolo is nothing else in effect – for sincerity; and the singer finds, when it is too late, that the tremolo has literally got him by the throat and he cannot get rid of it. This quivering of the voice, as if it were a jelly, may be due to a variety of causes. It may be caused by sheer affectation, or by unsteady breathing, or by fatigue, and occasionally by an elongated uvula. In the last-mentioned case a medical remedy must be found. Where, however, the tremolo is the result of mistaken ideas about the expression of sentiment, it must be rigorously corrected. In such work as

---

**'Musical Times A Hundred Years Ago' *The Musical Times*, March 1989.*

recitative, declamation, and *canto largo*, the voice must be firm and steady as a rock. If the voice persists in trembling, even against the will of the singer, then resort must be had to the practice of long, single notes. These notes must be done without any *crescendo* – steady tones, sung alternately *piano* and *mezzo forte*, and with a gentle, unwavering emission of the breath. Tremolo results very often from a wrong way of breathing; lack of sustaining power can be overcome by paying attention to the rules and suggestions already given [i.e. in his book]. Another very important point in connection with this *tremolo* voice lies in the proper 'placing of the voice'. If the tone is not directed towards the front teeth, so that it may be felt to vibrate across the bridge of the nose, then the voice trembles because it is not properly placed. As a last word about tremolo, it may be pointed out that all great singers preserve their voices much longer than the average artists, and while the latter usually show the tremolo, the former invariably never do. The deduction may not satisfy logicians, but it is sufficient for the student of singing.*

Reeves wrote perceptively, and from practical experience. But we must beware of assuming that *all* vibrato is suspect, just as we should disbelieve those who proclaim that no well-produced voice may be without it; for there are authorities on voice production who maintain belief in either one or the other of these creeds, implicitly and exclusively.

The truth is, surely, that vibrato is one of a number of valuable optional effects available to the well-trained singer. It has been so since sophisticated singing began, and indeed, before. Knowing, or rather divining when not to use it, is essential. Having the vocal control to take either course is imperative.

---

* Sims Reeves, *The Art of Singing*, Chappell & Co. Ltd, 1900, pp. 25–26.

# Some vocal cautions and counsel

### General

The following points are given in no significant order. The student is advised to consider them in the light of what he will meet and experience during the course. The latter section is not intended for the beginner, or the inexperienced. It refers to vocal application and performance, and is for the already active singer. Some terminology requires reference to the text of Section B.

- Practise often in front of a large looking glass, preferably with side mirrors for a lateral view.

- Do not hurry your development. The voice takes time to mature, and it takes time to eradicate any bad fault already engrained. Remember that even with a generally shorter life expectancy, serious singers in the nineteenth century, and before, were thought not to be ready for their public until their very late twenties, assuming a start made at about age twenty.

- Do not attempt vibrato yet. The aim is first to develop a perfectly controlled voice. When vibrato is desired, it can be introduced to an established and true vocal placement and technique. My exercises 53–55 should help when the time comes, after which move to other, more general treatises, or better still, individual tuition.

- As a general rule of basic style, aim at *legato*, *sostenuto* singing, as if, placing the violin bow on the string, you are playing a passage with one bow-stroke while altering the pitch with your fingertips on the neck. Make certain that the words do not chop the phrase up, but are incorporated into the *sostenuto* line. (Consonants must, of course, be clear.) Early music sometimes requires less legato, and a crisper transit; but *whilst taking this course,* for your vocal development and health, you should work only as suggested previously.

- Always encourage Mode Two* register to extend downwards in pitch, thus equalizing and smoothing the quality of the vocal instrument as a consequence of the resultant overlapping.

- Practise little and often. 'Sing often, but a little at a time,' advised the castrato Giuseppe Aprile, thought by some to have been the teacher of Manuel Garcia the elder.

- Never use a tape or cassette recorder to monitor your tonal quality, unless the machine is of exceptional capability, with excellent large speaker playback facilities, preferably separated from the machine itself.

- In conjunction with the points about pitch, on page 76, be wary when accepting Bach solo alto engagements. For various reasons, his solo alto arias often have a high tessitura. Before signing a contract, double-check the pitch to be used. The author recalls one unfortunate trans-Atlantic concert. He discovered too late that the pitch was to be $A_4=440$ after all. An already high (but just possible) solo cantata was thus rendered uncomfortable and unsuitable.

- Never forget that *all your tone* – Mode Two register as well as Mode One* – is to be thought of as emanating totally from the head cavities: the business area of the vocal tract lies above the larynx.

- Inevitably, the student will be concerned with the development of volume. Other than encouraging a greater flow to work on and in the resonators, and mentally to engage and 'open up' the cranial cavities even more, which will increase volume, there is an additional creative approach, useful for all voices. The bass-baritone, John M Hearne, a former student of the distinguished operatic baritone Redvers Llewellyn, tells us that Llewellyn was noted, during lessons, for reiterating: 'Your forehead – the point between the eyebrows. That's where the tone is. Now PULL!' Hearne writes, in an amusing and

---

* As will be explianed fully on page 25, Mode Two replaces the innacurate terms Falsetto/Head Voice throughout the course. Mode One replaces Chest Voice.

fascinating article, how he would pick a note from out there on the western horizon (the studio was high, overlooking Cardigan Bay) and 'pull it in and up' to that point between the eyes. Llewellyn would jab thumb and forefinger into his own forehead. 'Keep it there, boy!' he would growl.' It's got to resonate here.' He would bang the forehead again. 'That's where the place is. Natural sound box. Does it all for you. PULL!' And, as Hearne explains, in the 1985 *Journal of the Ernest George White Society*, the voice became bigger and bigger. The countertenor, whose timbres surely sound to depend so unquestionably on the cranial cavities in even more obvious manner than most other voices, would do well to remember Llewellyn's admonitions.

- *The median level, or note*. In a work of wide vocal range, the median level can be helpful. This is simply the average middle point, or note, of the work involved. For example, in a song with the large compass of:

over which the tessitura is evenly distributed, the median is at about E4. Sing with this area in mind as your centre of operation, of importance. Do not allow your voice to become too loud (which in fact is tantamount to losing essential equalisation) as you rise in pitch towards D5 or to become too discreet as you approach F3. A little practice with this approach should convince you of its value.

- Here is surely a particularly important piece of counsel. When basic vocal training is complete, be aware of the personal strengths and limitations thus revealed. Most certainly I do not advocate lack of ambition; but I underline that not everyone can be a professional soloist, nor is it desirable that all students aspire to it. 'In My Father's house are many mansions' would appear to be an apt biblical quotation here. Those with outstanding vocal and musical gifts, who are obviously full-time soloist material, should ask themselves finally, 'Am I suitable, psychologically? Am I thick-skinned enough?' (for example). The countertenor, for whom, in general terms, there will always be less (solo) demand than most other voices by the very nature of the musical repertoire, is advised to consider this especially. But if he really is outstanding, and is thought so by those best placed and qualified to give an opinion, then he should go for the top, single-mindedly.

### Not for beginners

- When seeking to extend the range, never force the voice. Forcing will almost certainly damage it sooner or later. Never be persuaded to work so hard that the larynx aches during practice, rehearsal, or afterwards. Coax and cajole your instrument if you wish to sing for many years to come. Misplaced tension produces a voice less loud than you imagine, and eventually constricts the tone, not amplifies it. Think of your head resonance at all times. Try to sing as if the voice does not actually touch the throat. This does not mean singing with breathy, unfocused tone!

- If a vowel on a high note is difficult to sing, do not distort it, but move to one more grateful to the voice; then, by stages, progress through the other vowels until you reach one which feels and seems to be nearest to that in question. Beginning with this adjacent vowel, gradually transform it. For example, imagine you wish to sing a high AY sound – something nearly always difficult.

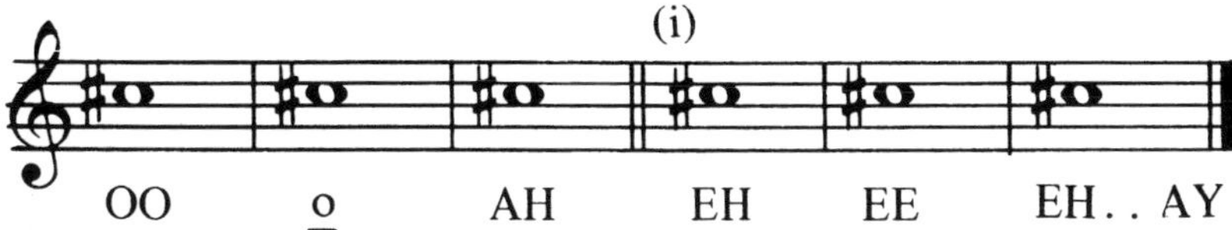



or better

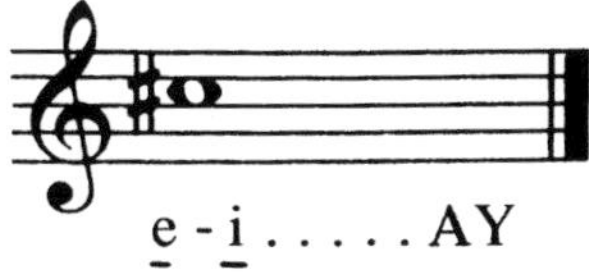

- Never shout the voice in search of some happier acoustic, especially in a warm, oppressive room. Such forcing merely tires the voice and uses it up. Instead, try to gauge volume, singing within yourself, using your own resonation and physical sensations as your guide. If, singing in a resonant hall, church or cathedral, there is a blurring reverberation, you must adjust accordingly. Too much volume will merely cause you to lose control of your tone. Better to sing more quietly, and feel the way, for the quieter tone travels more clearly in any case.

- Do not sing loudly for long. Never try to sing louder than is comfortable for your voice. To do so is to encourage eventual coarseness of tone and difficulty in producing subtler tones.

- While seeking to develop your lung capacity, do not go to extremes – like cramming in as much air as possible at all times. Take in what you need and no more. Overcrowding the lungs with air can lead to tightness, and eventually to forcing and inequality of tone; even, in bad cases, to congestion of vessels and tissues of the throat and lungs.

- When learning a high work or vocal part, be ready to do so using minimal volume and at an octave or some other interval down, at an easier pitch. Only when all factors are sorted out, attempt to sing it as written. (Even then, take care not to over-sing, or for long.) *Do not, of course, transpose exercises in this singing method, except as and when instructed.*

- When warming up, preparing your voice for use, do not be tempted to sing loudly: to 'blow hard through' as some singers call it. Instead, hum gently, encouraging the range to open up, using some of the exercises in this book. There is no need to sing at more than *piano*. Only when you have placed your whole range satisfactorily, should you expand the tone occasionally to *forte*.

- Approaching a new work, especially using Mode Two/Mode One register change, try first humming/singing through in a slurred *portamento*, almost as if drunk, to allow the voice to place itself gently and naturally.

- Yet never forget that sheer *competitive* volume is dangerous for reasons other than vocal health: it is an ogre which can destroy more than a single performance. Vocal equalisation and quality go all too swiftly. Upper Mode Two, and the *ponticello* area between and overlapping Mode One and Mode Two registers, can become strained.

- Resist the temptation to 'take on' roaring basses and competing tenors singing high in their voices, on full bore. Remember that their production (depending on the individuals concerned) might well be based on different criteria than yours; and that, anyway, head resonances make it unnecessary, and important not to push tone out. Try to ensure that any remaining imbalance felt, or commented on, is dealt with by asking the singers in question to sing more within themselves at certain points, or somehow persuading the director to adjust matters. This only applies to a very small group of voices indeed: we are not talking of a choir! Monitor yourself carefully. Solo, small ensemble, larger ensemble; all probably require some form of different tonal adjustments for loud, high singing. For example, one countertenor of the author's acquaintance has a voice liable to thin too much at *fortissimo* (not, I think, the result of tightening, but that of inherent vocal idiosyncrasy). This occurs in upper Mode Two register. He sounds as if he needs to allow his voice to bloom in this area, but he has a problem, and some other countertenors share it. It is concerned with intrinsic musical balance, with blend, with compliance. Like many countertenors, other than in solo work this singer sings for much of his time in smallish ensembles, and in a cathedral choir. The quality of tone appropriate for loud, high singing in one *milieu* is not always so for another, especially where microphone and engineers are involved. This problem sometimes seems particularly acute for countertenors, probably owing to the harmonics and formants of this voice. So adjust your tonal quality carefully. It can be distressing to hear playback of a track which is simply misleading and uncharacteristic of your voice, especially on a completed television or other recording, which, for various good reasons, cannot then be repeated while you adjust yourself vocally. The eternal problem is that of ensuring that you do yourself justice whilst keeping the director and producer happy.

- Whilst on the subject of recording, be watchful when there is only one immediate microphone of *diminutive size*. This often happens during television broadcasting – recorded or live. It is most dangerous in small ensemble. Despite the assurances of television engineers, if a voice of certain timbre is to one side of a tiny microphone placed at about knee level for invisibility, that microphone will probably receive too little of the voice in question; not merely in volume, but in timbre and quality. It can, if course, happen with other voices, but some types of countertenor are prone to suffer with this problem, again, probably, because of the particular harmonics, formants, and upper partials of this voice type. Singing more loudly will not help much. The recorded or broadcast effect will often sound starved and pinched, evoking the thinning quality emanating from a single channel of a highly sophisticated stereophonic recording when played through the tiniest speaker. Try if possible, to snatch a chance to hear part of the final recorded rehearsal and balance test, and if necessary, discuss (briefly) with the producer your relationship to the microphone and any shortcomings in the picking-up of your sound quality. Do this politely but clearly, or be prepared for disappointment later.

Television musical sound quality is known to be of secondary consideration, and can, of course, vary from mediocre (even terrible) to good. Unfortunately, the former is more often in evidence than the latter. Only when the singer is a celebrated or distinguished name, or when the programme in question is primarily a concert, and therefore the music is of prime importance, is it relatively safe for a singer to assume that he or she will be fairly served. If in doubt, investigate beforehand.

- Some are likely to disagree, but nevertheless I suggest that the following can be useful to check briefly:

    (a) personal intonation

    (b) personal tonal quality

*during rehearsal* when singing in a choir or ensemble.

Semi-cup one or both hands upright, thumbs next to the head, palms forward at right angles to the side of the skull, to extend the area and spread of the ears. Though a crude device, this is the nearest one can get to hearing oneself as the microphone or close-up listener does. It is useful not only to check *in situ* that your head resonances are as they should be, but also to enjoy the sensation, one might say the gratifying experience, of singing and listening to oneself at the same time. It is important, of course, not to over-indulge yourself, even during rehearsal, because it can lead to personal vocal idiosyncrasies or distortion and, not least important, can give offence to one's immediate neighbours in ensemble!

## Taking care of your voice

Acknowledging the sensitivity and sophistication of the vocal organ, it would be foolish to treat it badly and thoughtlessly. Much of the good work done during this course would be quickly undone, even ruining a well-trained voice forever in extreme cases. While not in any way advocating hypochondria, I feel that it is of the utmost importance to offer advice for vocal care, which is an important aspect of singing. We have dealt already with a few points. Here are more, gathered from personal experience and garnered from those of others. There is no special order, and much applies to all singing voices. Again the later paragraphs are concerned primarily with performance, and will not affect the beginner yet.

- Try to avoid singing out of doors. Apart from the effect of cold air on the throat and vocal tract generally, there is small chance of monitoring yourself outside. If unable to avoid singing in the open on some special occasion, sing carefully 'within yourself' at all times. Breathe through the nose as often as possible. Never shout; never *compete*. (That is a good general rule.)

- General consensus seems to advocate care when walking in cold weather. Ensure that, at the very least, your collar is buttoned. It is better to protect the throat (and possibly mouth and nose in extreme cold) with a scarf. If forced by circumstances to rehearse in a cold room, be prepared to wear a scarf loosely round the neck. The throat must be warm if good tone is to be produced.

- Inevitably, you will suffer sore throat or catarrh on occasion. Various gargle-preparations are available, but not many are helpful because the liquid cannot quite reach far enough. It is better to inhale, preferably using an old-fashioned china inhaler jug. *Karvol* capsules dissolved in boiling water are probably the best additive, but *Friar's Balsam*, or even just steam, are good too. A towel over your head, above a bowl of inhalant, is a reasonable second-best method. Many older singers and teachers advocate the use of the cold compress. Put a damp cloth round your neck at bedtime, covered securely with a dry towel. (Moist warmth is beneficial.) Lozenges are good only if they moisten the throat as well as gently disinfect. It is better to keep to long-tried, long-tested brands. Check the instructions. I prefer the freely available *Meloids* or *Fisherman's Friends*, but be careful not to over-indulge. Some singers foreswear the use of all lozenges. An old singers' remedy for an over-dry throat is sugar and water, or a little glycerine. Honey mixed with lemon is helpful too. Blackcurrant and glycerine pastilles are useful.

- If you have laryngitis from any cause, it is better to rest the voice completely, even if you seem able to sing or speak to some degree. In an emergency, throat sprays are available which can sometimes restore the voice temporarily, though timbre and range can prove uncharacteristic, and there is the possibility of delaying full vocal recovery. Normally, consult your doctor or chemist before using a throat spray.

- Avoid modern nasal drops that *dry* the nose out. As a singer, you must not allow any drying agent to interfere with the properly moist conditions of nose and throat. Nasal drops which act more conventionally, if they can be found now, should be used to unblock and ease the nasal cavities. If you have a cold, it is better not to sing at all if you can avoid it. Often, catarrhal conditions seem only too eager to move into the larynx and further into the sinuses. Using your voice tends to encourage this at such times, leading to loss of voice for a while. Avoid, for obvious reasons, 'drying out' cold cures and capsule treatments. They may suppress your cold symptoms for a period, but dry your larynx and vocal tract too.

- Do not shout or laugh loudly or violently. Be careful at parties or in any situation where there is loud music: it is very easy to strain your voice without realising it till the next day. *Remember that the non-singer seldom understands your problem*, so you should insist on moving elsewhere to talk without needing to compete. Keep your speaking light and placed high in the head.

- Until he abandoned most food or drink containing dairy products, and at about the same time came into contact with White's Technique, catarrhal infections had plagued this writer since early childhood. He is therefore able to comment on such infections with some bitter experience. Your doctor may prescribe a suitable antibiotic. They can be very helpful (used in conjunction with vocal rest, and probably inhaling) but do not put too much faith in them: they lose their effectiveness if used over-often. Always *finish* the course that has been prescribed for you. Antibiotics are not effective against viruses. Give up drinking milk, and eating cheese or cream during catarrhal infections. (Consider abandoning them completely, even when free of trouble!) As infected mucus begins to loosen, do not cough or clear the throat over-violently, in a manner likely to irritate and re-inflame the laryngeal ligaments, the vocal folds. Encourage the freeing and loosening with great care.

- Remember that the voice is a reliable barometer to your general condition. If you are overtired, your voice will probably be tired too, even before you sing. Get plenty of sleep. Take regular outdoor exercise, though not to unaccustomed excess. You are of course a vocal athlete. Keep yourself fit by guarding vocal and bodily condition, as an athlete would before a track or field event.

- As part of your regular diet, drink plenty of fruit juice, though perhaps not grapefruit or other edgy juices. The larynx itself needs fruit-moistening, but not irritants. Avoid alcoholic spirits and over-dry wines as a general rule. Drink beers by preference. Many laryngologists swear by Guinness! Port wine is also recommended.

- If you are a low or through-voice countertenor, do not be tempted to force Mode One register beyond its natural comfortable range, in the erroneous belief that you are developing or strengthening the vocal instrument. Preserve your nurtured sinus placements and balances: in short, conserve the benefits that careful work has given you.

- Try to ensure that any room in which you sleep has a minimal amount of clean-air access, but do not open the window more than fractionally, or even at all, in cold winter weather.

- If you are occupying a warm, dry room, it is a good idea to increase humidity by covering a radiator with a large, wet towel. This disperses moisture evenly in the air. In fact, water could be called the singer's friend, for the singer must preserve a moist vocal tract, though not a *sticky* one. During a cold, your body loses water through increased perspiration and evaporation, because of heavier breathing. Also, if you are forced to breathe through the mouth, each breath dries your lower vocal tract. You must increase your liquid intake. This will thin the phlegm that is forming inside you, helping to dislodge it gently, or disperse it discreetly because of its now thinner consistency. Water does this perhaps best of all. Ten eight-ounce glasses per day will suffice for this, to moisten dry, inflamed tissues of mouth, nose and throat. Eat water: fruit and vegetables are 80% water; fish is 75%; beef, ham and eggs, 50%.

- Always remember, in normal conversation, to ensure that your manner of speaking is gentle, in accordance with the vocal placing and consideration discussed and established during this course. Avoid heavy and guttural utterance, and careless, unthinking, coarse speech tone, whatever the natural Mode One characteristics of your voice. For the same reason, avoid attempting to sing low, heavy, bass notes, either for fun, for demonstration to bass students, or when rehearsing choirs. Also avoid careless use of high Mode One when demonstrating, or rehearsing tenor singers. Preserve your normal techniques.

- A good remedy for catarrh and hoarseness: 'Pour boiling hot water into a saucer, and let a large sponge suck it all up. Then squeeze it firmly out again. Hold the sponge to the nose and mouth, and breathe alternately through the nose and mouth, in and out.'

  'I sing my exercises, the great scales, passages, etc., and all the vowels into it, and so force the hot steam to act upon the lungs, bronchial tubes, and especially on the mucous membranes, while I am breathing in and out through the sponge. After this has been kept up for ten or fifteen minutes, wash the face in cold water. This can be repeated four to six times a day. The sponge should be full of water, and must be squeezed out. This has helped me greatly, and I can recommend it highly. It can do no injury because it is natural. But after breathing in the hot steam, do not go out immediately into the cold air.' (From Lilli Lehmann, *How to Sing*, 1914, p. 323.)

- Another treatment for catarrh: Mix equal parts of sugar, salt and bicarbonate of soda. Dissolve half a teaspoon of the powder in a half-pint tumbler of warm water. Pour a little into the palm of the hand and sniff it up the nostrils.

- Try homeopathic treatments for catarrh, especially Pulsatilla tablets.

- If you enjoy swimming, take care not to do so in a swimming pool whose water is strongly treated with chlorine: it can affect your throat. The sea, with its helpful salt, is far preferable to a singer for very obvious reasons. Ensure, of course, that you choose a known clean beach.

- Avoid singing in tobacco fumes or excessive dry heat. Even breathing and talking in such atmospheres is inadvisable, but it is sometimes difficult to avoid. If forced into such situations, drink as much water, or comparable liquid, and take as much time in clearer air as possible (though not abruptly cold). Try to avoid breathing dust. It is probably unnecessary to say it, but do not smoke at all, yourself. Avoid sleeping in newly-painted rooms: paint-fumes often affect the throat. So, too, can aerosol sprays, like deodorants and polishes. Be careful of charcoal fixative, or hair lacquer.

- High-voice singers are likely to be more easily affected by irritating troubles. Countertenors are no exception. This is not normally a slur on their technique, but is because the delicate edges of the vocal folds are more readily affected by outside factors or careless treatment. Never forget that, however inhibiting, sensible precautions must always be taken if you wish to preserve your voice at its best. Remember that, unless you have an agent, or other individuals concerned in some direct way, only you will be particularly interested in your vocal condition or care in the days and hours before the concert. The first concern shown by anybody else, if at all, will be just prior to your appearance on the platform.

- When rehearsing, especially on the day of the performance, develop a technique that keeps the director or conductor happy but does not use up too much of your voice. Preserve full volume jealously. Give him, of course, a few passages at full strength, so that he may gauge balance and effectiveness. Do not give *performances* to an empty hall, only to find yourself at second best for the real thing, later. Insist on a decent gap and proper rest between rehearsal and performance. You will almost certainly find more understanding of this abroad, out of Britain. For some reason, the singer receives far less consideration in this country in matters of this sort, unless of course he or she is a celebrity.

- Never make the mistake of assuming that a lengthy total vocal rest will leave you ready and able to resume a heavy singing schedule after it. Keep your voice gently moving during any lay-off (other than for laryngitis). Use humming and the odd exercise daily throughout your holiday, then gradually build up your practice again till you are ready to sustain your normal schedule.

- Before a performance, avoid all violent exercise or recreation. Do not practise or perform immediately after a heavy meal. Allow at least one hour. Many singers avoid peppery food, for this can inflame or irritate the throat. Do not talk too much, or even at all, before performing or practising at length. Refrain from talking while travelling in trains and buses: dust can affect sinuses and larynx, and noise will inevitably encourage you to talk louder than is wise. When driving alone in your car, never vocalize too loudly: remember that a vehicle counts as a hot, dry, small room with obvious vocal dangers!

The advice above is general. Undoubtedly, you will meet singers who habitually ignore or even scorn some of the points made, and, what is more, seem to thrive! For how long they will remain unaffected is not, of course, foreseeable. In any case, everyone is slightly different. I can only underline that in my experience, and that of many others, the points I make are important, and the advice good. For detailed vocal health and care, *The Singer's and Actor's Throat*, by Norman A Punt, is recommended (see Booklist).

Somebody once wrote, very perceptively, that a singer is a dual personality. He or she is never without thought for their alter-ego, never happy each morning, even on a rest day, till the state and condition of their other self is ascertained. If this puzzles you, you are not yet a singer!

# The teaching, or otherwise, of vocal registration, and how it affects the countertenor

There are more differences of opinion on registers than about any other vocal subject. Even though they are dealt with later during this course, often in detail, let us consider the main approaches made by teachers, noting as we proceed that countertenor singers and teachers are to be found in groups one, two and, of course, four.

A first group, we shall say, favours an approach which sets the register system out in detail, and makes the student aware of it and its essential application to his or her own voice individually, at the outset. All development takes place with the register framework in mind.

A second group uses an approach which does not acknowledge registers; or, to be more accurate, proceeds *as if* they do not exist, encouraging, developing and employing the subtlest of adjustments to achieve ease and range.

A third variety could not differ more, though at first glance it might seem similar to the second. These teachers believe quite literally and totally in the non-existence of registers. They claim that the human voice comes from straightforward action in the two vocal folds, activated together, and that there is but one legitimate vocal tone as a direct result – for male voices anyway. High notes are difficult if the vocal folds are thick; low are problematical if the folds are thin. Therefore, range is simply prescribed. Anything above this single voice is 'falsetto, which is not a real voice, and its use is inartistic, even contemptible'.

A fourth group, almost the equivalent of the third but not quite, could be said to exist within the ranks of countertenor singers and teachers. They cannot and do not, of course, dismiss all other voice types as illegitimate; but say that for themselves, as singers, in effect no register system exists within their range: no subdivisions, no adjustments. Mode One is ignored, even abhorred, and unused, even though it exists, and is usually employed when the singer speaks. It can be seen, therefore, that the criteria of group three, discounting their views on falsetto, of course, apply more or less equally to this group four. It consists of those who, whilst asserting that the countertenor is a one-register voice, insist that in its rarity this single register possesses no Mode One – even vestigially – and that there is probably no possession and certainly no employment of falsetto of any kind. Extreme elements of this subdivision seem to maintain that all falsetto is incapable of variation and manipulation: it is a single state. There is therefore a sideways glance at group three.

A fifth, and sizable body of otherwise sound teachers share the view of falsetto demonstrated by the third school of thought – usually in connection with the male voice only – but are aware of the subtleties of the vocal mechanism, so they fully support and teach the register method.

This seems a good moment to underline that the pejorative term 'falsetto' is a most unfortunate one, implying, as it does, an unnatural usage. It is nothing of the sort. Theoretically, every voice-type, male and female, has the ability to produce this mode. Musical fashion plays a part in our attitude to all this, and 'falsetto', better thought of as Mode Two, seems to have been used variously and expertly over many centuries in many cultures.

The truth is that, seen in one way, every different note of the vocal range and scale is a register in itself, requiring a different adjustment. Considered thus, therefore, there are as many registers as there are notes in the voice, but that is not easy to demonstrate practically and effectively in a treatise such as this. We must then be content to work in larger, if (and this is inevitable) simplistically conceived, areas – or the usual registers – in the present course. For though examination of the method which follows might suggest otherwise, in my usual practical work with students I try to imbue the multi-register, note-by-note adjustment – that used by the second group. I teach, in general, as if the registers do not exist. This is, of course, the method and teaching of White's Technique. Yet I back this up, *where necessary,* with reference to vocal subdivisions by sensation and using conventional terms. Some students, and their particular situation and problems, seem to need more detailed use of register terminology; but ideally, I believe it is desirable to employ it only when absolutely necessary for understanding, and for practical reasons – always with qualification. Naturally, so far as training the alto range is concerned, the procedure with the through-range man differs slightly from that with the (apparently) one-register specialist.

However, because this present practical course is communicated using the printed, not the spoken word; and by means of musical notation, not demonstrated sung or hummed example; also because it is likely to reach the widest variety of users and perusers imaginable; I have adopted the following scheme.

I begin by describing the acknowledged chief vocal areas, or registers, of the human instrument. Thereafter, I use these crude but useful labels for easier identification as we proceed, but hope to encourage a considerably more subtle conception of the human voice as the course develops.

It will be noticed that throughout I employ the terminology vocal folds, not cords, because the former is the exact translation into English of the *Nomina Anatomica** term, plicae vocales.

---

* *Nomina Anatomica* is the revision of the International Anatomical Committee appointed by the Fifth International Congress of Anatomists, held at Oxford in 1950.

# Historical vocal colour and its implications for the singer today

It is very important to realise that in the very timbres and varied colours of the registers and vocal placing, and their sophisticated employment and control – remembering that vocal training was expected to occupy many years of intense study – we have the material and means with which the pre-nineteenth-century singer created and painted his myriad effects. Most late- and post-nineteenth-century teachers and singers seem to have been encouraged by the tenets and influences of the Romantic movement, and the advent of the non-creative type of mechanistic approach to voice pedagogy and production, to banish many such colorations and subtleties in the interests of volume and/or uniformity of tone-colour throughout the range. This approach changed, even transformed, other instruments too, especially the organ. Because the early, Baroque, and Classical singer had at his disposal far more genuine variety of tone than most of his successors, and because such variety exists not only within each particular historical school (and there are several main schools with which to deal), I have had to tread a carefully balanced path in this course. Yet I hope to have hinted to the student the great importance of eventually developing appropriate singing techniques and styles for the music he will meet in his career. This, I feel, is best prepared for by not pushing him too far towards any one particular period or style.

Should all singers of early music today be prepared to study and master all the many vocal styles expected, historically? It depends on each singer's circumstances and ambitions, but one is left with the impression that many otherwise excellent singers, often involved with early music exclusively, do not use enough varied tonal coloration, or elasticity of style. Perhaps there is a fear that a voice possessing genuine choice of colours and timbres may be confused by some listeners with the uncontrolled, accidental and disturbing abrupt timbre changes of most untrained voices.

So we in the early twenty-first century have the most difficult task. A musicological super-awareness of centuries of music, and anxiety to perform earlier schools in their proper and characteristic manner (an awareness and anxiety seldom held in the past), dictates to the singer either the development of an ability to deal with all, or most, periods of vocal music; or, instead, to specialize strictly in one century, period or school, and to stay within it.

Whichever option may be settled upon, one would hope that the student would feel keen to begin at least some little study of each period and its styles, having established his basic technique via the present method. Properly, even essentially, any intensive study decided on should be undertaken at the *conclusion* of this vocal course, during the process of which the student is at least pointed towards many of the main areas of imperative historical study.

As a postscript, perhaps, I ask the more experienced reader to consider this. Of the five teaching approaches already referred to (pages 19–20), which seem more likely to achieve or allow for the appropriate timbres needed for the various periods of earlier music, and which for those of more recent date?

One thing seems certain or self-evident: any teaching method which proves itself closed and incapable of allowing later development of further colour and effects, in response to the demands of some particular vocal period and requirement, is not advisable.

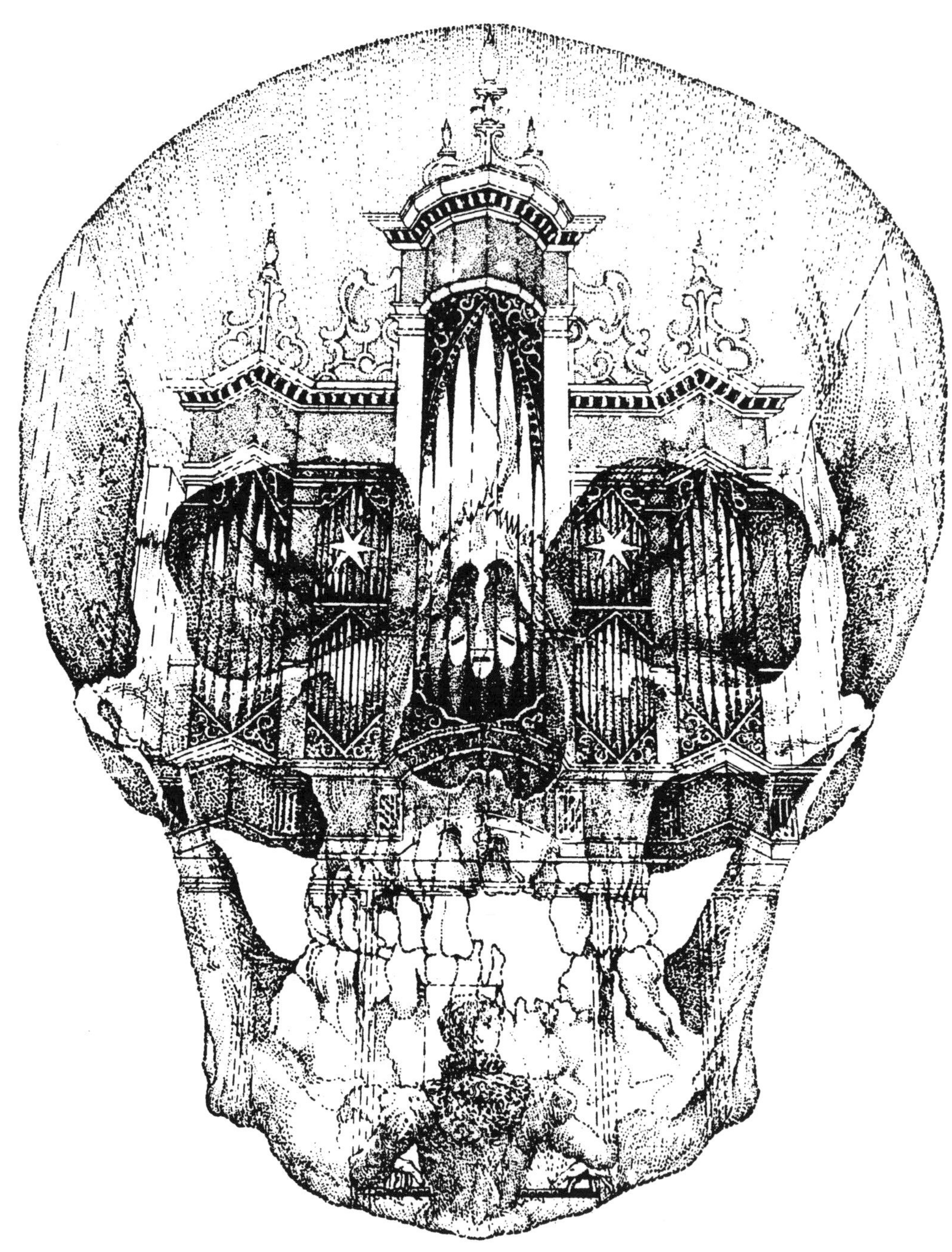

'Taverner' an etching by John O'Connor of obvious relevance to the vocal student.

Before starting practical work, we must first acknowledge the minefield which appertains to vocal terminology. Fierce differences of opinion exist on the subject, and a short treatise cannot deal in great detail with it. Nevertheless, it is essential to explain the main points with the countertenor singer in mind, as he prepares to begin the course.

Our most accessible – and main – vocal register, which can be called Mode One, 'basic', 'foundation' (but hopefully not 'chest voice'), is possessed by everyone, male and female. Nobody can fail to be aware of it. It is our basic sound. Unless some sort of vocal abnormality is present, we speak in Mode One. Therefore, it is usually the first register in which we attempt to sing. It is capable, in some, with development, of the powerful, rich, low and medium-low tones of a bass or a contralto. On the other hand, it can also produce the crudities of the brutal high shout which, used *en masse*, produces the football crowd roar – when the larynx is *forced* high.

Mode Two is our secondary vocal state. For most people (if they develop it at all), other than facilitating their scream as an infant, use of Mode Two is usually acquired later. It is often termed head register, or less happily, head voice. Adoption of this colloquial misnomer, as with chest voice, is misleading but understandable. Just as Mode One seems to produce resonances and vibrations in the chest; so, when using Mode Two, the singer experiences higher, lighter, disembodied sensations in the head.

Unfortunately, this confuses the issue. The reason is that all voice, *all* phonation, actually *originates* from well above the chest. When a cathedral, church or concert organ is being played, especially when loudly, it vibrates the building, particularly the lower notes. Feel the walls! But they are not the instrument. It is useful to think of the head as the organ and the body as the gallery or screen on which it stands. Try singing in your Mode One register. Feel your chest! It may be a bit early to feel sensations in the head, but a little later in the course we will be looking to discover and develop vibrations in your cranial cavities.

Therefore, use of the terms head and chest, attached to voice or register, is not only wrong but liable to cause misunderstanding and problems in various ways.

The countertenor is concerned mainly with the development of Mode Two – unalloyed, or 'pure' head register – the origin and technical constitution of which has been much disputed. Only since the nineteenth century does head register seem usually to have been confused with 'mixed voice' – that lovely effect employable for softer, higher passages, especially by the modern tenor. To achieve it, Modes One and Two are engaged simultaneously on the same notes. Historically, it should be remembered, the two main modes or registers were considered separate, though in need of relating closely to each other. Early in the nineteenth century, for the male voice, mixed voice came to be the one way of achieving this.

The term 'falsetto' is yet another misnomer which, unfortunately, the countertenor cannot fail to have met already! Yet it is simply unalloyed Mode Two – falsetto/pure head register. It is capable of at least some development in almost everyone, so there is nothing quirky, strange or *false* about it. What it does have about it is an undeniable, disembodied sensation and sound, which is retained and even enhanced when developed to expert proficiency. In fact, this quality is part of its *raison d'être*.

Of course, when undeveloped, or used poorly by unenlightened vocalists, Mode Two can be its own worst enemy, and it is easy to see why the term falsetto has become ingrained and pejorative. Genuine Mode Two is not to be confused with weak, almost timbre-less, undeveloped falsetto, or with a loud but unfocused hoot. Mode Two/pure/unmixed head register is a resonant, focused, sophisticated *supported* falsetto. It is far from untrained, unrealised, 'collapsed' falsetto, which can indeed sound false and fake.

We shall return to this in more detail, but initially at least we shall be using both Mode Two, and light, upper Mode One to develop appropriate countertenor tone. The Mode Two specialist need not fear this for, if desired, use of Mode One may be discontinued later. This one-register countertenor – not the extremely rare variety with no Mode One at all –

seems to be most common in England today. Nevertheless, it is to be hoped that more 'through-register' countertenors will soon be in evidence for musical and historical balance.

Because the student must already be aware of the physical sensations and general pitch of his two main registers, I do not yet propose to enter into discussion of their physiological origins. The student will encounter this later in the course, and *The History and Technique of the Counter-Tenor* is recommended for even greater depth.

As we move into practical work, I underline that use of Mode One for the countertenor is always light, and employs the upper, more veiled, quality within the area:

as explained later.

## Resonance

First, we shall need to focus most attention on the various and many head cavities, including the mouth spaces. While, obviously, activity in the vocal folds plays an important part in phonation, it is the resonators which build the superstructure of overtones recognisable as a well-produced voice. Mental image is all-important whilst the voice develops. It help place, and coax into being, tones in the correct adjustments. Familiarise yourself with the position of the main areas of resonation in the head. Feel your skull. Experiment. See the illustrations on pages 28–30. Try to examine a real skull, preferably in section.

Should you doubt the huge tonal capabilities of the head cavities, consider this. The rising of stomach air through the oesophagus, into the mouth, may be used to demonstrate. Such air, caused by flatulence, may be converted into a belch of enormous tone, even of slightly varied pitch, and ringing intensity, by focusing and allowing it to resonate in the sinus system and mouth cavity. This vulgar but revealing capability, which may be used to form clear, controlled words, serves to illustrate a crude tone achieved without the help of vocal folds. But unlike stomach gas, air from the lungs encounters the vocal folds en route. The combination of folds and resonance produces the singing and speaking voice.

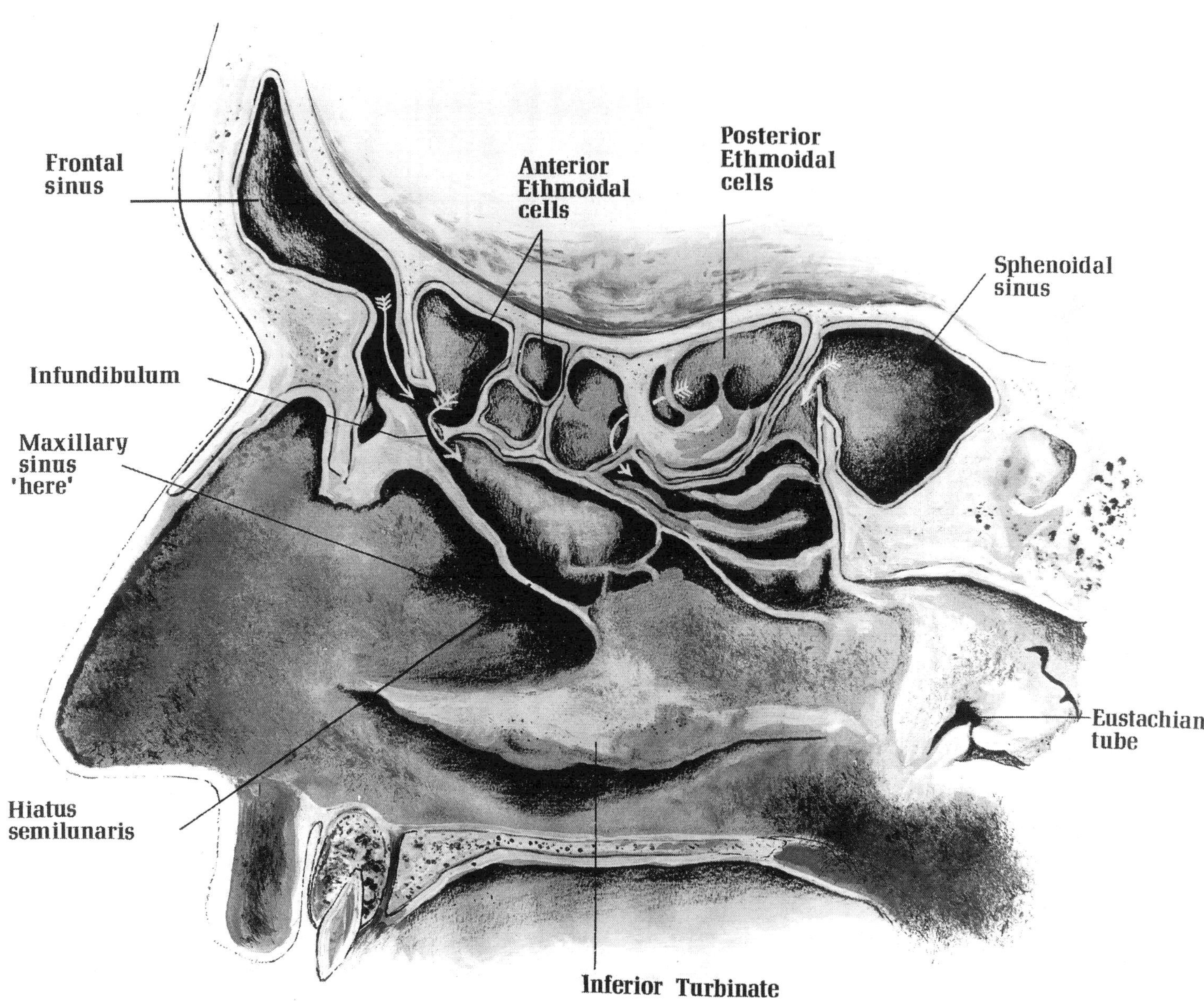


**Figure 1** Right side of the sinus system.

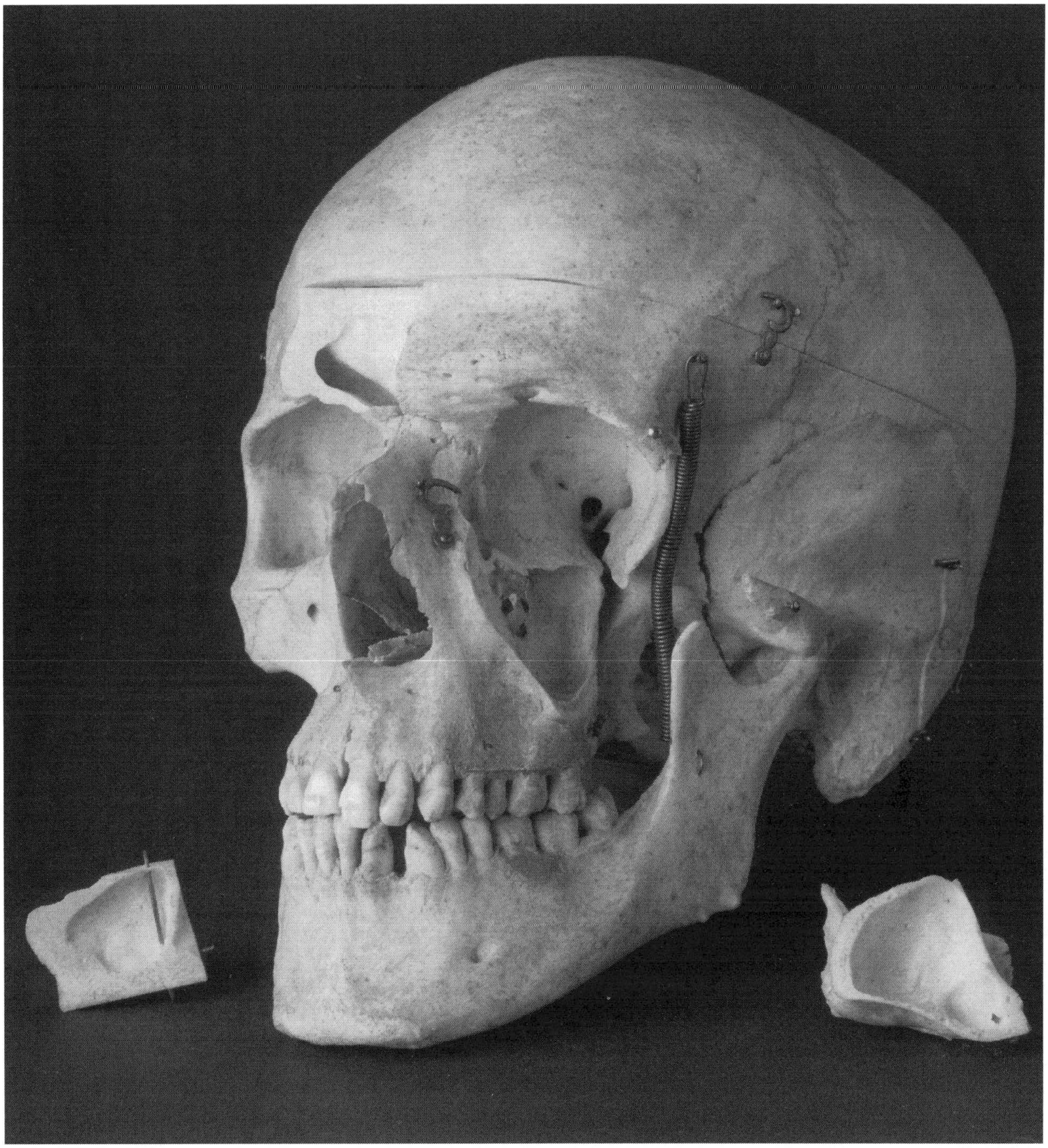

**Figure 2**  Skull with maxillary sinus and frontal cavities revealed.

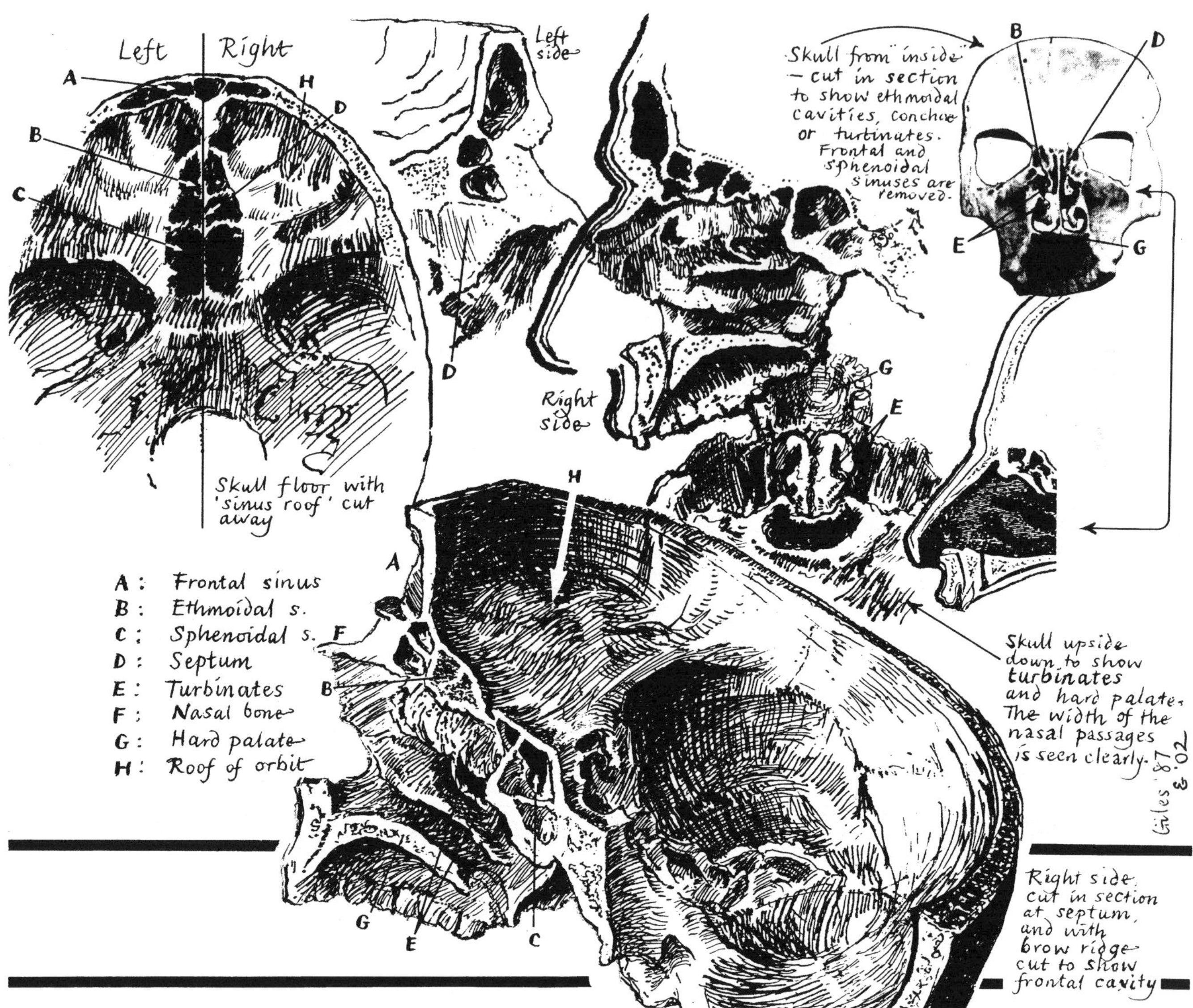


**Figure 3** Cranial cavities, nasal passages and palate.

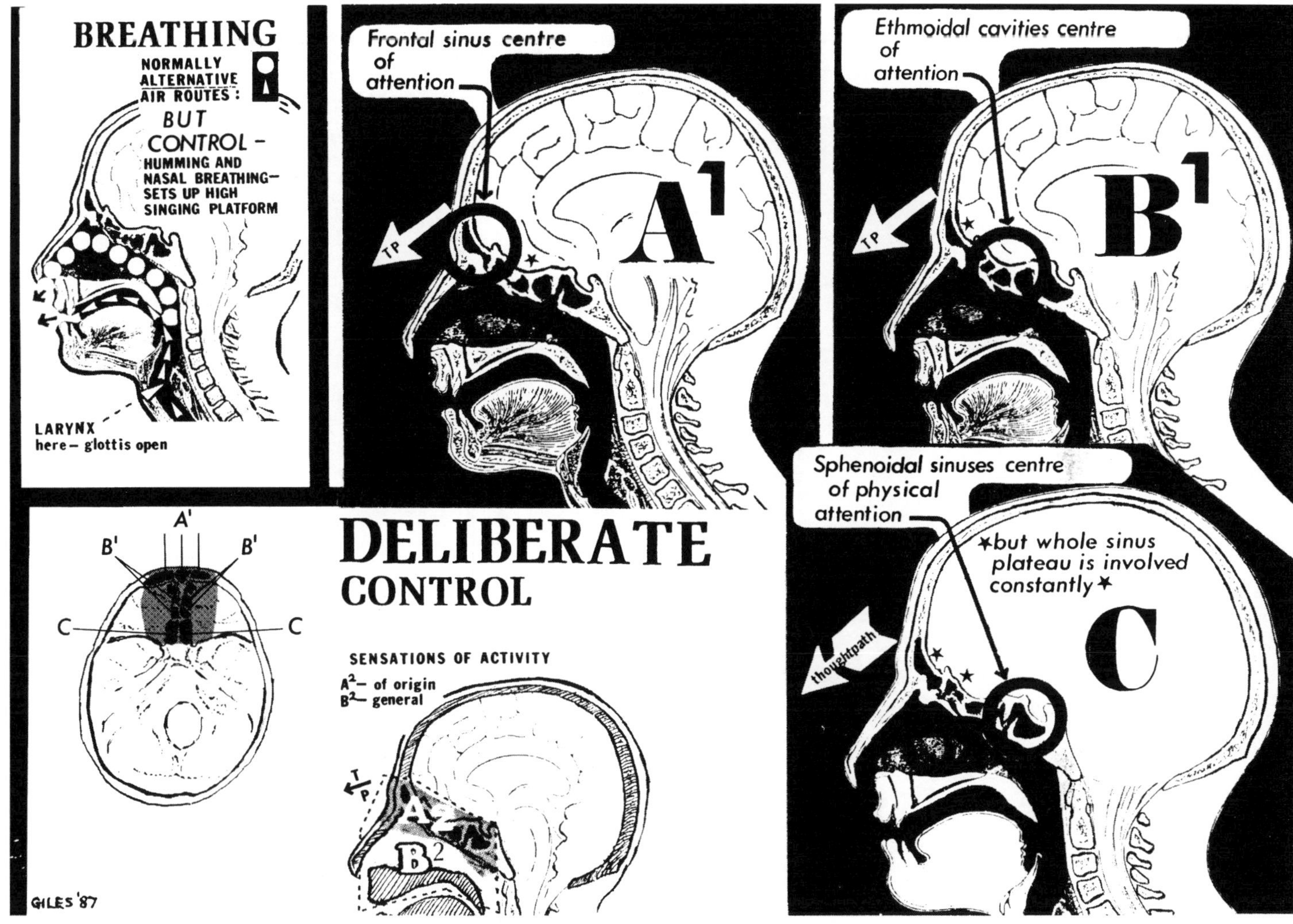


**Figure 4** Sinus areas of sensation and focus.

### Key to abbreviations in the exercises

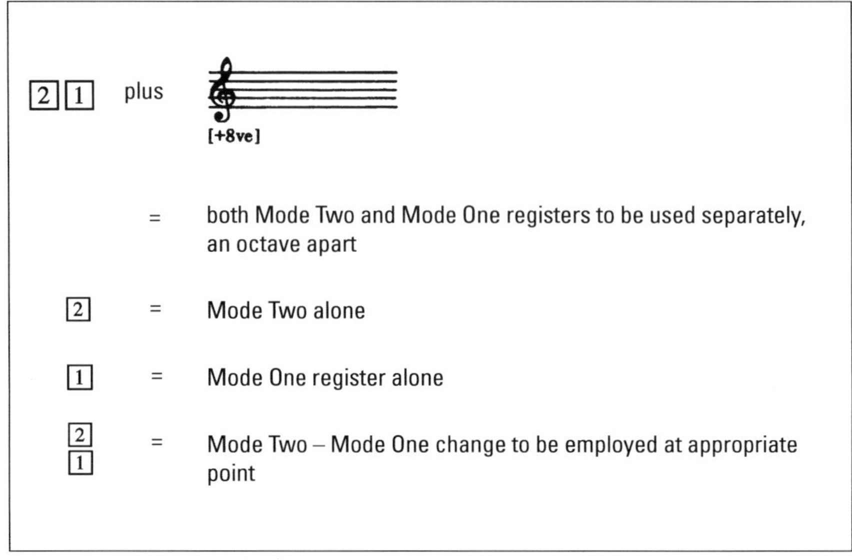


|  |  |  |
|---|---|---|
| 2 1 | = | both Mode Two and Mode One registers to be used separately, an octave apart |
| 2 | = | Mode Two alone |
| 1 | = | Mode One register alone |
| 2/1 | = | Mode Two – Mode One change to be employed at appropriate point |

### Practical work

Place this book on an upright music stand, at a height correct for a balanced level head position, whilst you are sitting on a straight, hard dining chair. Sit up in a balanced, upright position. While concentrating on the skull diagram and your own head in particular, hum a Mode Two / falsetto note in the easy region of:

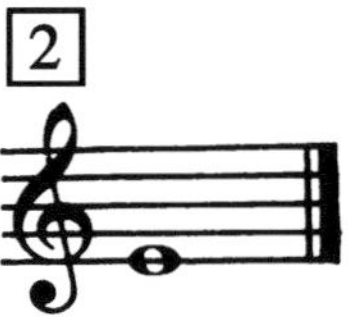


Do not strike a piano note or concern yourself with exact pitch, but *hum gently, using natural, normal breathing*, on this arbitrary note. It must not be the tight-lipped, forced, competitive 'choral' hum. Encourage and experience sensation high behind top teeth and inside sinuses above. Visualise the full range of sinus cavities. Encourage the hum to pervade all of them, particularly the frontal sinuses. Spend several minutes exploring these sensations, then try the same an octave below, in

Mode One. Hum – phonate gently, *tasting* the hum, experiencing, savouring it in both Mode Two and Mode One, concentrating especially on the nose bridge and above, high forward and high back. Experiment with tongue placing at this stage. Now allow the mouth to fall *slightly* open, loosely, and try to retain the hum sensation. Keep the tongue high against the palate momentarily, then flatten it down, tip behind lower teeth. Still try to retain the hum sensation and the feeling of activity in the head cavities. Repeat several times. Do not attempt to *sing* as such. The correct hum placement is to be a very important key to development, and something of its sensation should always be present from now onwards. There must be no force or effort employed, except mental concentration. As an alternative, the hand-hum – produced by blocking the slightly open mouth with the hand – is useful. Then try a gentle AH sound. The AH should veer towards UH. Always imagine your note as *emanating* from high in the head cavities and forward in the skull, as if vibrating air were flowing down from a high point, like a tap switched on, high up; air never rushing through the mouth. We are in search of a lofty *control* location. Do not try to push the sound outwards, for it will radiate inevitably once you have produced it correctly.

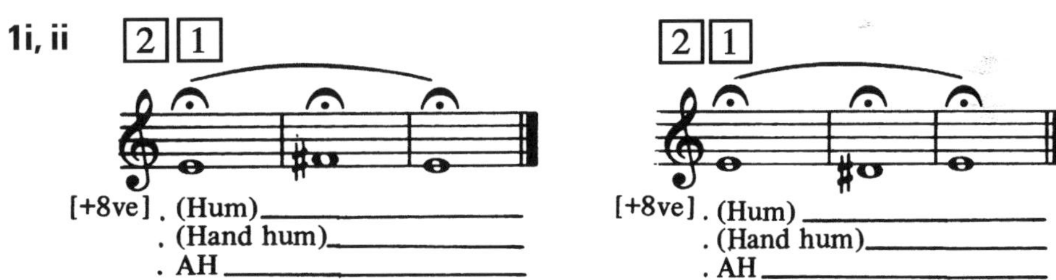


Now raise your chosen note to pitch as shown, not by thinking up but by thinking forward slightly, though not forcing or pushing. Return to the first, thinking slightly back again. Movement of the two notes is to be considered horizontal on an already high level. Work only *piano* or *mezzo piano*. Next try the semitone movement as shown. Then open your mouth slightly and sing both figures quietly on an AH sound. Retain all the previous feeling and resultant vocal placement experienced.

Should you be finding difficulty in retaining the high frontal sinus placement, try bending double, hum, hand-hum, then sing MA gently

**2i**

to:

followed by MEENEE MEENEE MOH (as in h<u>o</u>t), or preceded by N. Try cat-like MEEOWS to a similar sequence of notes, perhaps slightly higher in pitch, singly, then slurred over the whole phrase. Now sit upright on the chair as before. Your vocal placement should be improved. Remember to work all exercises sitting for the time being. Balance, posture, and correct ease help focus attention where it should be: in the head.

**2ii**

**3**

Another helpful exercise is to pinch the nose bridge several times while gently phonating, perhaps bending double as in (i) and murmuring:

A first exercise in volume variation. *Broaden* the tone by letting it pervade the ethmoidal cavities after a gentle start in the frontal sinuses only. Do not *push* the voice downwards in pitch. Begin now to yawn gently a *little*, as you produce tone; but do not allow the mouth to open over-much. This is essential for the establishment of sinus awareness. The student should keep this in mind from now on.

### The Italianate vowels

These are by common consent the purest and most musical for the singer, therefore most suited to the formation of sound technique. Retaining what has been achieved so far, try the following vowels. Note

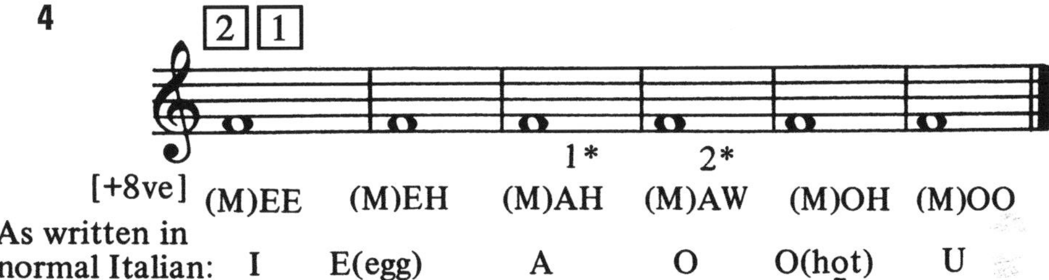


which, if any, still do not seem focused high, forward in the skull and vibrating slightly round the nose bridge. Keep the tongue as flat as possible. Begin AH, EH, EE; then as shown.

**(1*  with a strong tendency towards MUH in Southern English)**
**(2*  something between MAW and MOT in Southern English)**

Vary the pitch slightly for 4, between D4 and F4. Keep your tone gentle and steady. Do not move on till *all* these sounds resonate in the frontal sinus areas, particularly for the 'higher' notes. Be conscious of broadening – thinking the tone into the ethmoidal cells, mouth only moderately open. Remember that for some time yet we shall be working at little more than *mezzo piano*. Volume will develop from this discipline. Later, you will be encouraged to sing more loudly and to use the ringing tone this method brings. Until that time, persevere with small volume.

If the vowel AH still refuses to emanate from a forward high position (a problem sometimes encountered by English students), try using, instead, a southern (M)UH (as in cup), or (M)EE. Leave AH until later. Work exercises at *mezzo forte* or *forte* for the present. In short, free yourself of vocal inhibition before attempting to develop your control and skills.

**5**

In the above exercise, move slowly, trying not to alter the shape of the mouth dramatically for each change, nor yet to open the teeth more than or even as much as about one finger width. Vary the pitch slightly within the exercise, but make only semitone or whole-tone movements. Sing gently without accent. Concentrate on 'filling out' your resonating cavities. Use the following exercise similarly after working it first as

**6**

(followed by N before each vowel)

indicated:

Do not attempt to vary the outward position of the lips over-much in this or any other exercise until directed. Do not use a keyboard for accompaniment till the use of one is indicated.

**7**

i.   Hum/hand-hum the exercise through.

ii.  Sing gently to MAH, then AH and the other Italian vowels.

iii. Now sing it at various pitches between these extremes.

At this point, the student may wish to use Hewlett's *Think Afresh About the Voice* (pages 62–3) for additional simple exercises in voice placement. In any case, it is a good plan to re-work our exercises 1ii–7, rethinking and re-examining the movement of the voice, high forward and high, less forward in the sinuses, gently pinching the nose bridge and touching the forehead and temples with the fingers to encourage

**8i**

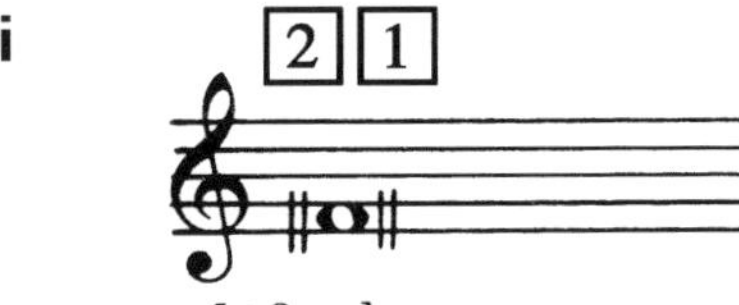


vocal placement.

### Vowel practice using Italianate Latin

After humming and placing the note, intone on it these Latin phrases, smoothly and softly, mixing them in varying order or sequences:

(a)  Meum, meum, meum, meum (*meh-oom*)

(b)  Mene, mene, mene, mene (*meh-neh*)

(c)  In nomine, in nomine, in nomine (*een-naw-mee-neh*)

(d)  In manus tuas, in manus tuas, Domine (*een-mah-noos-too-ahs-*

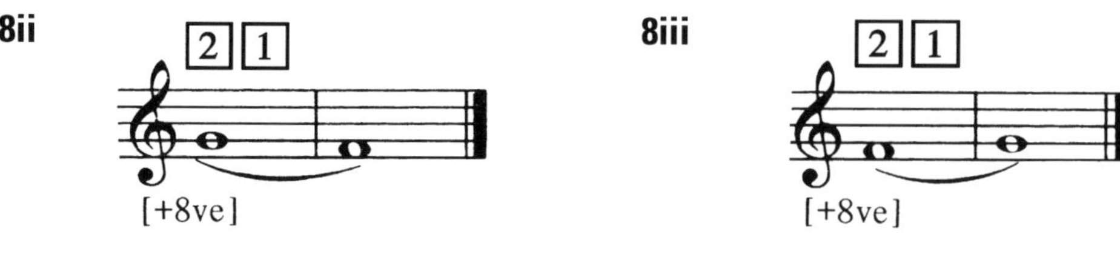



*daw-mee-neh*)

Now vary the pitch of the note in comfortable range, Mode One, then Mode Two. Try to match their tone qualities. Remember your sinus placement. Work between B3 and A4.

Similarly in exercises ii and iii sing phrases (a) to (d) on the notes provided, remembering to shift sinus placement forward or back as the pitch rises or falls. Vary the pitch. Repeat the notes as often as needed to accommodate the verbal phrases.

**9**    Now apply and adapt the Latin phrases in exercise 8 to exercises 1–7, mainly but not exclusively in Mode Two. Seek, as always, to encourage a firm – not loud – quasi-Mode One tone in Mode Two, and Mode Two bloom and subtlety in your lightly-used Mode One.

## Vowel practice using Italian

**10**   (a)  l'inganno, l'inganno          (*l'een-gannoh*) (as in h<u>o</u>t)
         (b)  quando difende              (*qwahn-daw deefendeh*)
         (c)  rammento, rammento     (*<u>r</u>a-men-taw*) (roll the 'r')

Work this exercise as in numbers 8 and 9. *Do not allow the consonants to be firm yet.* Still working from an upright sitting position on a dining chair, the student should by now have reasonable control over a modest area of both Modes One and Two, plus the ability to apply basic Italian vowels, and a few Latin and Italian words and single progressions, to comfortably-placed short musical phrases. There should be little or no consciousness of the activity of the vocal folds. They will have been performing their function automatically. Think then not of the larynx but of the head cavities, as if all tone actually *originates* in these resonance chambers. Keep the frontal sinuses working to preserve bright tone.

**11**    Exercises 11i–11xi are to be hummed, hand-hummed, then vocalised quietly to the various Italian vowel sounds, MAH initially, then EE, EH, AH, AW, OH, OO in order. Do not change vowels note for note. Vary them only as indicated.

Despite appearances, these, and all exercises in the course, must first be mastered at an extremely *largo* speed. As you negotiate the intervals and slow running phrases, watch to avoid pushing or vocal tightness. In the exercises following, dotted lines sub-divide the phrase occasionally.

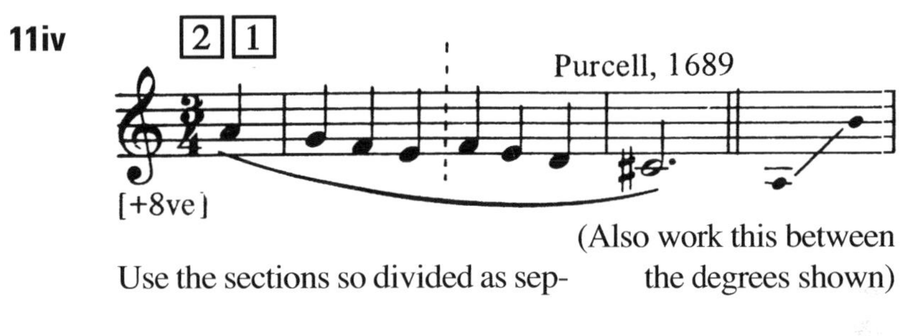


Use the sections so divided as sep-    (Also work this between the degrees shown)

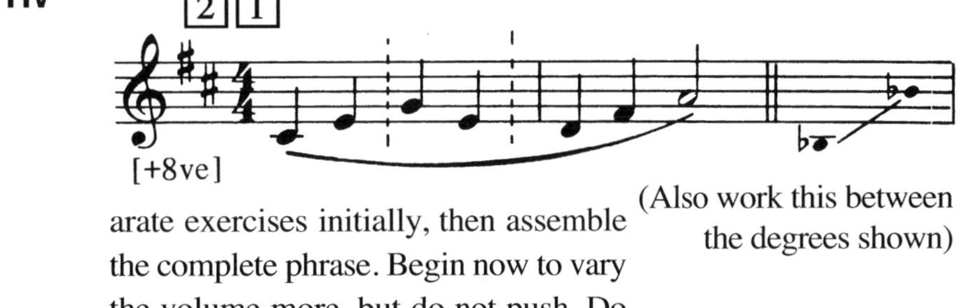


arate exercises initially, then assemble the complete phrase. Begin now to vary the volume more, but do not push. Do

(Also work this between the degrees shown)

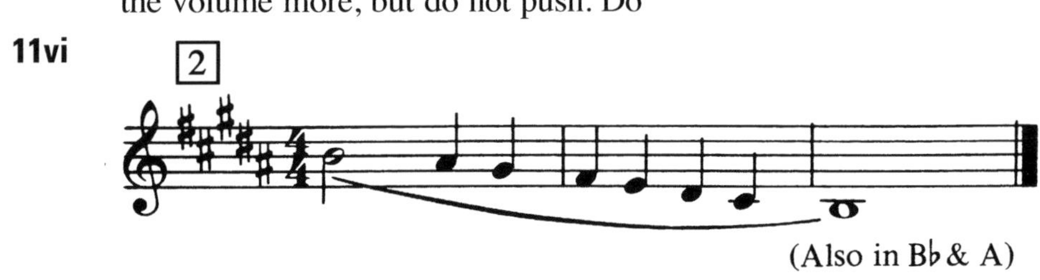


(Also in B♭ & A)

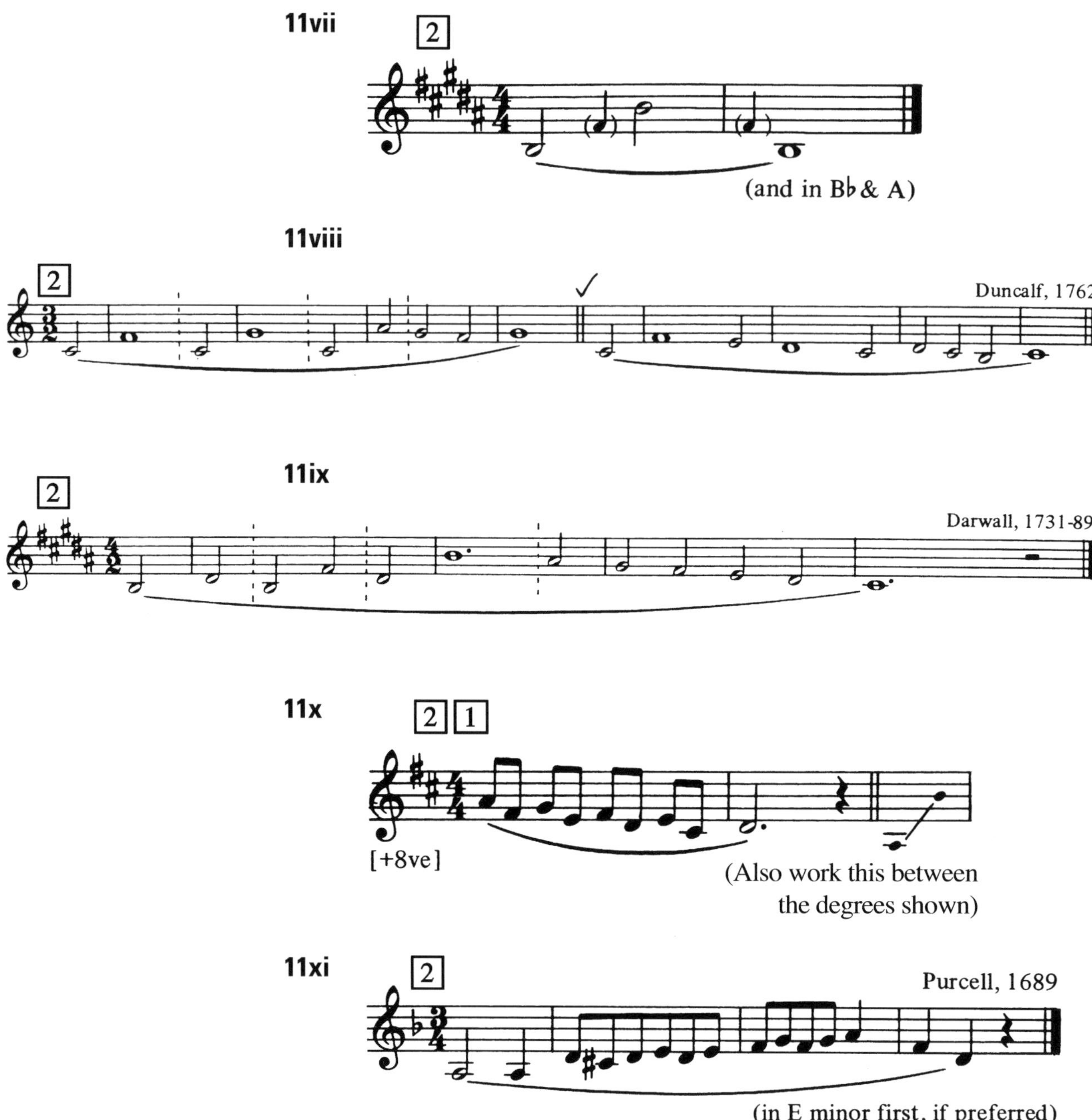


not attempt to switch registers within the exercise. Sing to one vowel throughout: AH; then EE, EH, AH, AW, OH, OO, tackling them in that order.

Now stand, feet slightly apart, body balanced evenly on both legs, head level. Repeat exercises 6–11, checking your vocal placing. Do not move on till the correct resonation and placement are present while you are standing to sing. As a valuable alternative, try all exercises so far using N instead of M, lips slightly parted. Retain this option as the course proceeds.

### Breathing and breath control

So far, the student has been breathing naturally, as for considered speaking, but now he will need to begin the development of greater capacity and technique. Certain other published singing treatises provide excellent methods for this, and as the countertenor is really no different from other singers, it seems unnecessary to provide here more than a few useful points with which to begin. Initially, begin to take in more breath now, and remember these points:

(a) Avoid breathing through the mouth. Whenever possible, inhale through the nostrils. The nose purifies and warms the air before reaching the vocal areas. The whole vocal tract needs to be warm for the production of good tone. The nostrils must therefore be clear and free. (See Section A, Some Vocal Cautions and Counsel). Breathing constantly through the mouth inclines to dry the throat and make the voice husky. It is of course impossible to sing certain fast passages without breathing through the mouth. One cannot always breathe quickly enough through the nose during a snatched semi-quaver rest without an audible sniff! The singer must exercise common sense.

(b) Never heave or jerk the shoulders in the act of taking breath. There should be no obvious sudden body movement, except that the ribs should expand sideways, the chest rising and falling with each phrase. Abdominal breathing – during which the abdomen protrudes in inhalation while the diaphragm is considerably depressed – is used by some singers. This has been termed 'yawning' technique. Another method is termed the 'retching' technique – not as alarming as it sounds – in which the diaphragm is raised more and the abdomen strongly contracted. The yawn method is compatible with the general approach made in this treatise. The student should return (much later) to these matters, consulting C Kennedy Scott, and Gardiner, for example, but exercises 12–15 should be found useful. For a detailed description of no less than six breathing techniques, see *Voice and Song* (Butenschøn and Borchgrevink, pages 54–55).

**12**   Practise inhalation before a long looking glass to correct faults arising from defective breathing or facial expression. It is useful to practise other singing exercises in front of the mirror.

**13**    The following exercise is useful, daily. Close the mouth. Inhale, long, slowly, gently, to full lung capacity, but only full – not forcing in any way. Hold the air in the lungs for at least four seconds, then exhale at the same speed, via the same method that you used to inhale. Do not practise this for long at a time. Two sessions of five minutes, with a ten-minute rest in between, is suggested as a maximum.

**14**   I am indebted to the late Frederic Hodgson for a valuable and ingenious, but simple, variation of the last. Whilst walking, especially up hills or stairs, hold the breath for say four paces, and then release it, exhaling over four paces. Then re-inhale rapidly and repeat. Gradually increase the amount of paces accordingly. This has the added advantage of being workable at any time, and easily appraised and measured. Freddy, who for many years was an alto lay-clerk in St George's Chapel, Windsor, used to employ this practice daily before evensong, while climbing the outside stairs to the castle.

**15**   Be warned that to *cram* your lungs with breath can result in tightening and loss of vocal control. To convince you that full lungs are seldom necessary for most singing, try breathing out until no air whatsoever remains within you. Then 'sing' without breathing in first. The sound will be unpleasant, but you may be surprised. Some more breathing exercises, best left until much later in this course, are included on page 107.

Except, possibly, for special effects introduced after a basic technique has been established, the lips should not be shot out abruptly like a trumpet bell. Tone produced indiscriminately via such a mouth-shape can sound contemptuous. The student is advised to absorb the following:

(a)  Always consider that vowels are the result of *interior* cavities, their forms and, where appropriate, their adjustable shapes. Mental attitude is thus very important. But certain lip formations can be a subtle help and bring extra, specific colouring to already formed tone. A *slight* lip movement forwards, like a shallow trumpet bell, is in any case important for the forward vowels EE and (Italian) EH, and used occasionally in others is sometimes beneficial. Only the experienced singer will be able to judge when and where.

(b)  Remember that the tongue should be as flat as reasonably possible with comfort during normal singing, its point behind the lower teeth, Keep the head level and still.

(c)  Later, when you wish to study and perform earlier and specific schools and their tone colours, their techniques and specialised effects in depth, then you may need to adjust the basic approach outlined above. A much *busier* mouth (still with a relaxed musculature) may

well need to be employed ultimately. The exploitation of historical vocal tone colour in its varieties is something which must come later, following completion of this present basic course.

## The introduction of expression and volume expansion

Work these exercises sitting down in the first instance, and then stand upright in relaxed, but balanced, position, taking care to retain the same vocal sensations.

---

*Much later in the course, the exclusively Mode One countertenor may well adopt a slightly tilted head position forward for his very lowest notes, in similar fashion to, and for similar reasons as, the bass singer approximately one octave below.

Exercise 16 should also be worked starting on $E_4$, then $F_4$. Omit the last two notes when practising the phrase in Mode One. In the above *messe di voce* exercise, use contrasting volume but without losing sinus placement or acquiring roughness or harshness in the *fortes*. Change from one vowel to the other must be sudden and distinct, the mouth remain-

**17**

ing almost still. Hum and hand-hum first, *thinking* the vowels. In this and other exercises requiring volume on low Mode Two notes, think the tone wide and broad as you move down. Retain the high head resonation at all times, never allowing the frontal sinus area to cease its contribution. Do not force or grate the larynx in your quest for volume.* Think of your ethmoid and sphenoid sinuses filling with sound,* deepening as you engage more and more cavities and cells. Imagine the air to be *flowing* through, not merely vibrating. Even visualise it not as air but liquid.

**18**

In exercise 17, each note is to be sustained, i.e., is to be level without any swell in the middle. The phrase is to be *legato*. Keep the voice quite steady. At the pause note, let the voice taper off in body of tone but remain full and un-thinned. Drop down *portamento* to the octave below. Stay in Mode Two throughout, with full quality. Sing *mezzo forte* or *forte* except at the $B\flat_4$ on and at the drop. Then reverse the dynamics, being careful not to force to tighten the low note.

---

* Especially in Mode One, that is, when working in the octave below.

Sing exercise 18 lightly and reasonably quickly, in a single breath. Retain the sinus placement even at speed, so begin work rather more slowly. When confident, vary the volume somewhat and introduce the stresses. Sing everything evenly, firmly, but with no *staccato*, one quality of tone throughout. Do not allow yourself to force at the stresses, but allow tone to blossom in the resonation cavities. Start the first note firmly, though un-forcedly. Have your mouth open in position before sound occurs.

## Mental reversing of scales and arpeggios

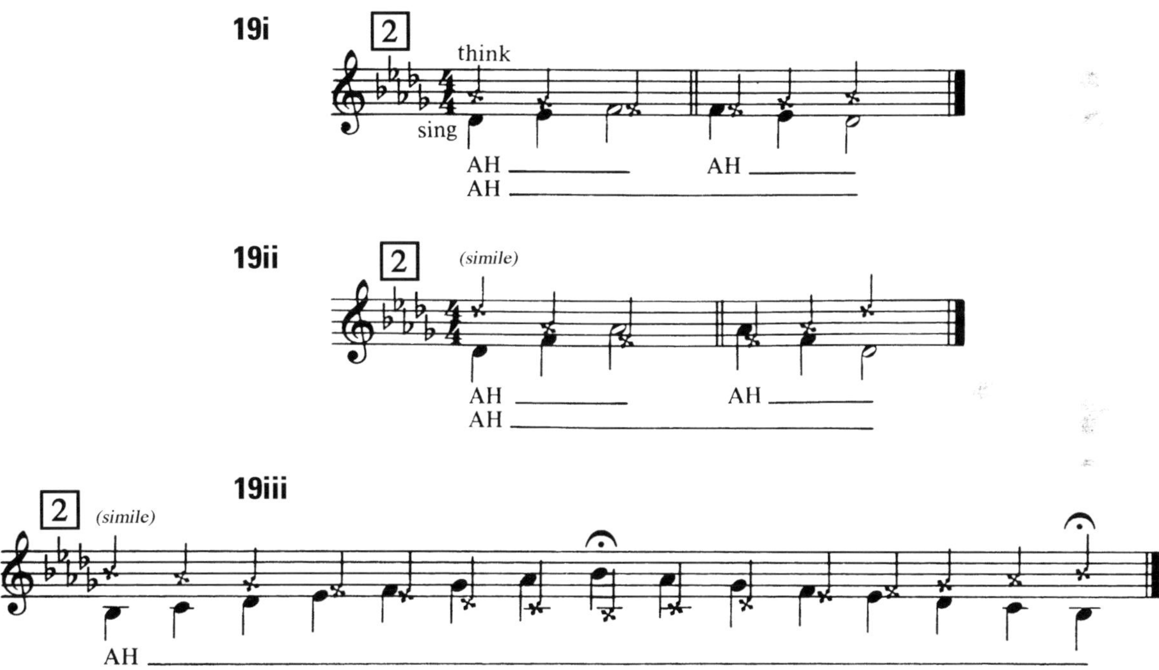


This is another useful and creative approach towards the attainment of mental control. When ascending or descending in pitch whilst singing, visualise a downward and upward movement in direct opposition to the apparent rule: up = down, down = up, as indicated below. The voice reacts increasingly to mental stimuli as you develop. Anything is welcome that helps you to overcome difficulties which extension of range, up or down, brings to all too many singers of various voice types. Your

**20**

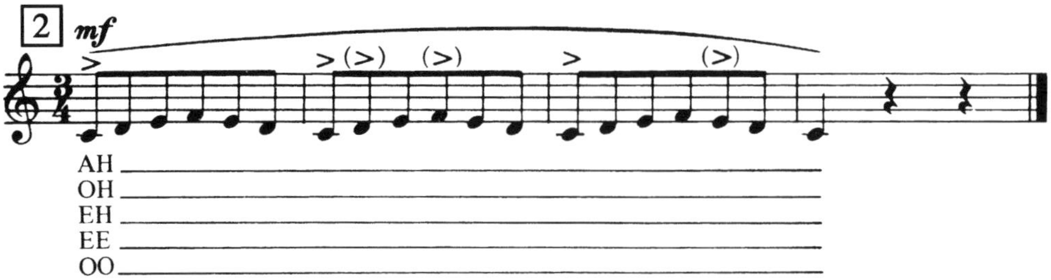

**21**

sinus control, of course, should already be working for you. Exercise 19

**22**

will help consolidate your existing mental control and inspiration. Keep both in mind as you work all exercises from this point onwards.

The exercises following are designed to practise volume expansion and

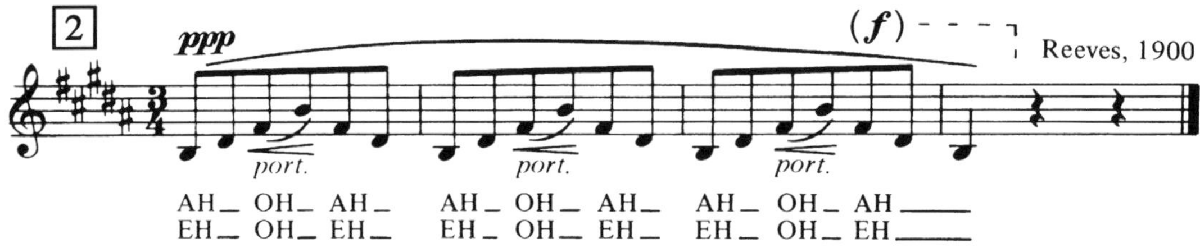


Reeves, 1900

**24**    expression, plus mental scale reversing. Sing them *slowly*, without

stresses to begin with, breathing at each bar-end to allow the mental reversing to become established, till you are able to manage all aspects together.

**23**    Exercise 23 helps smooth and refine transition from lower Mode Two to upper Mode Two. After it, particularly in the middle and lower areas, Mode Two should have achieved something of the strength and resonance of Mode One. (We shall soon be considering register-negotiation in detail.)

Sing the complete passage *without* stresses to begin with, taking care not to push at the topmost note. When the stresses are included, do not push that highest note: *allow* more sudden tone in a quiet context. Use AH and OH. Follow general directions from exercise 18. Watch for any tendency to flatten thirds and fifths. Sing *legato*, almost slurring the notes. For exercises 18–22, ensure that after a slower start, you sing lightly and quickly to cultivate refinement. For lowest pitched notes, do not be tempted to try for strong tone by pressing the chin hard against the throat. Do not move the head about. Sing these exercises (18–22) only in Mode Two for the present.

Up to this point we have ensured that the two main areas of operation, the modes or registers, are totally related but not joined. The student could now choose whether or not to concentrate only on Mode Two, leaving Mode One alone entirely. As a general rule, the light type of voice, which often has potentially a higher Mode Two range than the average, might well develop into a particularly high countertenor. For most people, nature and musical aim are together the deciding factors. The aspiring high countertenor – usually defined as one who extends, and stays, at almost all times in his Mode Two – may now wish to move to exercise 33, but is suggested that he at least read the next section through.

### The full-range voice: developing Mode Two / Mode One change

It seems impossible to help the student with this development without some detailed explanation. I make it purposely without physiological description, but in language and terminology already employed. As we are not yet ready to consider the action of the vocal folds, but are concerned with the resonators, we shall begin with these considered in relation to simply-experienced registers. (Vocal-fold activity, of course, is important, but is dealt with in some detail in Section D.)

The sinuses express visually the physical *experience* of registers. Hewlett writes:

> We can see why there has been disagreement about how many registers there are. Before the time of Garcia, it is said, two registers were usually recognised; since his time, three. Some have postulated four, some insisted on one only; a perceptive writer considered that 'one register is not a starting point but a goal'...If we make a broad distinction between a voice with or without a strong sphenoidal component, we can so define two registers. A voice which could distinguishably add to pure from sinus activity,* first the anterior ethmoid cells then the posterior, and finally the sphenoid sinus could be said to have registers. My own experience, both in myself and in most of my students, points to three. I have not been able to detect a subdivision of ethmoid cell activity, * but the three main components of the sinus system, namely frontal, ethmoid and sphenoid cavities, are distinctly identifiable in practice.†

Mode One has a useful sub-division: its upper area can be gentler, softer and more lyrical. It is this quality which some countertenor singers employ regularly. As mentioned earlier, the lyric tenor 'headvoice' of today is usually a skilful, sometimes unconscious admixture, on all notes above E4 or F4, of upper Mode One and medium Mode Two, with generally more One than Two in the mix. It is actually the mixed voice. It is not pure head register, though is often referred to as such, incorrectly. The lighter the tenor, the more Mode Two is present in this mix. There is, of course, a distinction between Mode One resonated mainly in the cranial cavities, and true Mode Two, which is produced not only

---

* This is better thought of as vibrations within the sinus system (PG).

†Arthur Hewlett, *Think Afresh About the Voice*, page 75.

in the cranial cavities but by a shift in laryngeal mechanism also. The pre-Duprez, pre-Heldentenor, lighter, historical tenor, seems either to have used a very light mix with a preponderance of Mode Two, or, sometimes, genuine Mode Two. There were slight variations, country to country.

Although, again, there might have been slight variations at different periods, the historical countertenor, alto, or *haute contre*, clearly seems to have been a vocal range or ranges which used *unmixed*, expertly developed Mode Two in one, two or even three adjustments or subdivisions. (Development of these will be explored at a later stage.) In many cases, the light upper Mode One was added, but not mixed, except momentarily at the register join, to produce a continuous vocal range of great versatility. This type of countertenor, using only one, or rarely two, Mode One adjustments, is best defined today as a low countertenor. The high type usually has as great a range but is lighter (usually, at least), pitched rather higher, and does not employ Mode One as a general rule, either because the repertoire does not require very low notes or because his Mode Two has firm power low down.

Both high and low varieties of countertenor can produce a voice of great flexibility and resonance, though neither usually possess the sheer power to rival the volume of the stronger full modern tenor, except in the upper vocal reaches of the countertenor range. Today's light lyric tenor, a descendant of the pre-Helden type, is comparable, however: though not, it would seem, of the same timbre as the pre-Baroque, Baroque or Classical tenor in most European countries except perhaps Italy, which may have favoured use of light Mode One to a higher point than in other places.

To summarise, then:

(a) High countertenor: Mode Two only, as a general rule, but with the option of employing basic or light Mode One.

(b) Low countertenor: Mode Two plus upper Mode One.

(c) There is, in addition, another, extremely rare, ultra-light lyric tenor called *tenor altino* or *contraltino*. This voice is considered low countertenor also. We shall return to this in a moment.

I would underline that these categories are rather simplistic. 'High' and 'low' seem to suggest extremes, which are in fact misleading at times when we are considering range. They are better though of as *specialisms*.

Again, to summarise, if the tenor's voice is a *splice*, the usual low

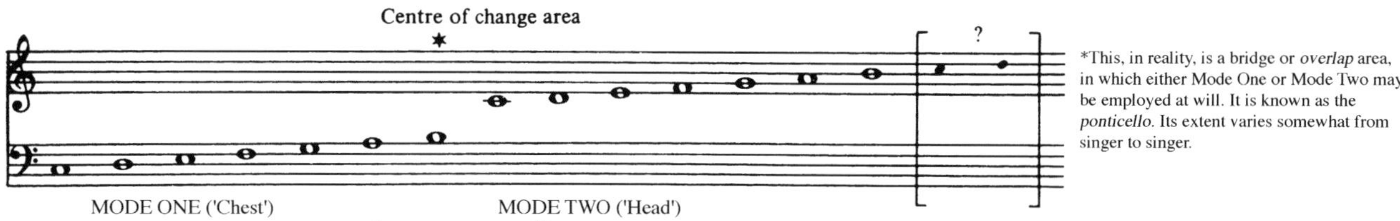


*This, in reality, is a bridge or *overlap* area, in which either Mode One or Mode Two may be employed at will. It is known as the *ponticello*. Its extent varies somewhat from singer to singer.

countertenor's is a *dovetail*.

When we reach them, the next exercises are especially for low countertenors of either type, but the high variety may use numbers 25 and 26 to help extend Mode Two down in pitch, and would normally ignore register-change directions. But for low countertenors, as for the tenor range (to which all low countertenors are related), the register-change mechanism is all-important. (Not that continuous, conscious monitoring should be sought.)

The Modes One/Two change area for most low countertenors will probably be found as indicated in notation:

While some heavier voices may feel the change a little lower, some lighter ones may feel it appropriate a bit higher – even perhaps up to E4, like a tenor; even higher in the case of the extremely rare *tenor altino*. *The student is warned not to be self-deceived*. Remember that what counts in the end is comfort, musical effectiveness, and vocal health. Proper sinus placement of the voice will reveal its laryngeal tendencies almost automatically.

It must be admitted that for many countertenors there is even amusement, and at the very least a marked lack of enthusiasm, for using Modes One/Two change; partly as a result of their own, and often other musical people's misunderstanding of the historical background. There seems to be an odd fear of 'cheating'. For the same reason, the modern tenor will seldom admit to the use of what he considers mere falsetto.

---

* In theory, contraltos and mezzo-sopranos should make good teachers of through-voice countertenors, though with a few notable exceptions such seems not to be the case, so far. Even though female and male voices are at roughly similar pitch in this instance, with roughly similar register changes, the eternal problem appears to be that of a low-sounding voice teaching, and demonstrating, to develop a high voice in the male student. And, historically, it seems extremely unlikely that male singers were taught by women until the nineteenth century (except, perhaps, privately in some cases). It is, of course, fair to say that many non-specialist male teachers today are not good with countertenors either, but for different reasons.

Yet, in enjoying and exploiting the resultant available tone colours, women singers use their several registers naturally and unselfconsciously,* just as the male voices did before the mid-nineteenth century. Over-obsession with totally identical tone quality throughout the range seems to be a nineteenth- and twentieth-century phenomenon. This applies equally to instruments. The voicing of the pre-nineteenth-century organ, of all dates and schools, is a thought-provoking example.

But much male solo vocal repertoire can be negotiated without the change. Such change is, by admission, an added difficulty, and (for today, with its eagerness for instant results) it has the disadvantage of usually taking longer in training. But persevering with through-voice technique has obvious advantages; and, logically, eschewing it seems similar to a string player ignoring the possibilities and contrasting timbre of his lowest-pitched string. It all depends on the musical goal of the individual singer. One thing seems certain. Most modern countertenors are called on, like it or not, to be far more musically versatile than their historical specialist forebears probably were, on the European continent at any rate; though the situation in England seems likely to have been more elastic. Today, unfortunately, most of us cannot usually afford to be too specialist. The high and low labels, therefore, are perhaps more broad indications of intention.

For the development of the all-important mental approach, as well as for the sake of convenience, most exercises in this section are shown at tenor pitch, i.e., the sound expected is an octave below the printed note. Study exercise 25i. The student who feels *genuinely* happier with a higher centre of change area should employ it. In exercises 25–31,

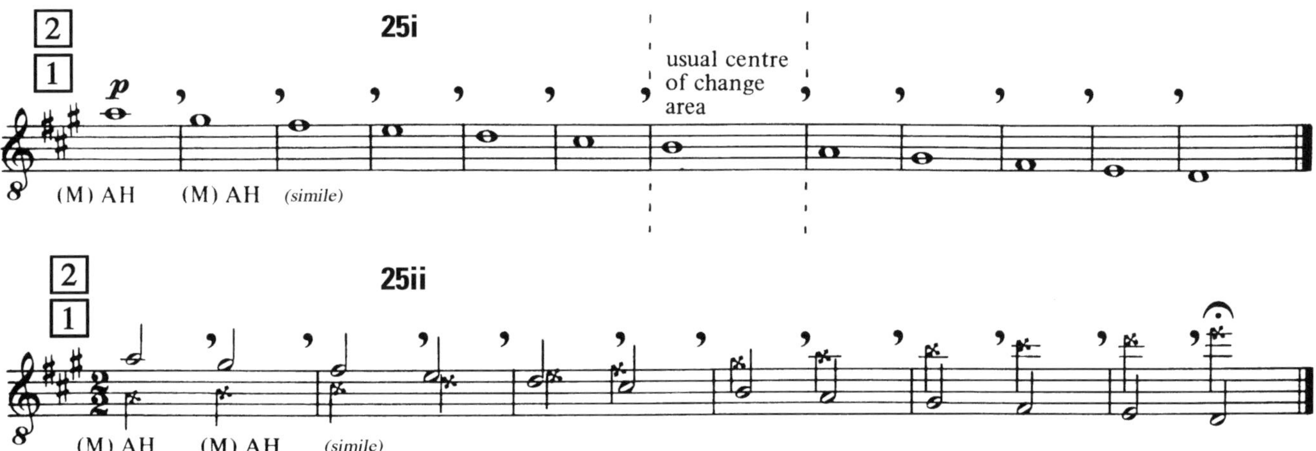

therefore, adjust your approach to suit any alteration of centre. Make this decision with great care; monitoring yourself at all times to avoid damaging the progress already made, and indeed the voice itself. Begin work on the following exercises sitting down, as before. Try 25i and 25ii initially without recourse to the detailed directions which follow; but in 25i, during the process of moving from A3 to D3, be conscious, as always, of working horizontally across the sinus table, frontal–ethmoidal–sphenoidal; thinking of medium- and low-pitched notes as placed so high in the cranial cavities as to make it impossible for them to be higher. Then try 25ii using the scale-reversal image:

Thus we have employed two different mental approaches to the same exercise. Ease of transit across the registers may or may not have been felt in one or other version, or indeed either. Now consider the following points before attempting it again. As always, it is a good plan to hum or hand-hum the exercise before applying the vowel. Initially, in both its versions, this 'descending' exercise is first to be sung to a single vowel, AH, softly and slowly, stopping after each note. If either version seems to be a more effective way of negotiating the register change, concentrate solely on it until it is well established, then try the other. In your eagerness to make a smooth transition (Mode Two to Mode One in conventional parlance), do not allow the bridge area to fade tonally. Subtlety is one thing: *evasion* is another! Whilst experiencing, but not dwelling on, the sensations of passing over the 'break', be conscious of equalising or matching the tone – a capability you should have developed already. Each note must be steady before proceeding to the next. Work with gentle perseverance, often, rather than for a long time, using the hum frequently.

Try the exercise to all the Italian vowels; but the high-placed forward AH is to be most important. Keep the volume *piano* throughout. The break may seem too obvious, though in some voices it may already be minimal; but if there is still a marked difference in tone, return to some of the earlier exercises. It must be emphasised that the break is quite another matter, and usually still to be expected at this stage. Do not force Mode Two so low that it is tightly *pianissimo*: let the change occur naturally, when Mode Two is becoming less effective. Always remember that the change will occur in an area, not on a specific note on every occasion it is sung. The point of this will become increasingly obvious as we proceed.

There is a third approach which may well be unnecessary in the case of some students in whom sinus and mental control is well advanced. In the following exercises, an imaginary note (∗) has been shown to help prepare the voice to move smoothly into the next register. Creative images, in some form, are part of the mental, not primarily physical approach, which we are pursuing. A third such image might be helpful.

It can be seen that in one sense, if (1) the almost horizontal flow of notes across the sinus table, together with vibrational activity in adjacent cavities, and (2) the contrary direction principle of the descending and ascending scale are effective, this thought-note is merely a back-up method of mental control. Though different otherwise, all these control images/approaches have one thing in common: they free the larynx to do its job automatically. This is true particularly of sinus control. The

big difference between pure sinus control and the other two is that considerable evidence exists to suggest, strongly, that vibrational activity in the sinuses and head cavities is not merely a mental image which takes attention from the larynx but is a physical phenomenon. We may therefore refer to it as sinus tone *production*.

Think of, picture, the thought-note while still phonating that immediately before it. In every case, the thought-note precedes the change of register directly, so the asterisk signifies this too. This note has no timing value, and is not to be sung. The pitch of exercise 26 may be varied slightly to suit the individual.

In this exercise, and those following, some singers may wish or need to bring the thought-note and change into operation rather earlier (see the

**26ii**

paragraph preceding exercise 25). Hum and hand-hum through first. After MEH-NEH-MEH, attempt an unforced, bright MAH vowel. Sing each three-note phrase separately. Always approach the upper Mode

**27**

One notes with high forward resonance and placement prepared. While the change of register will never quite be eliminated, both you and your eventual audience will cease to think of it. It will sound, and it is, a quite

**28i**

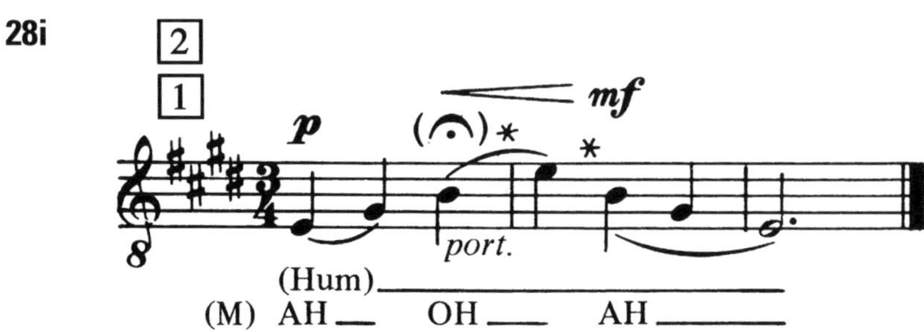

natural progression; in much the same way as the equivalent in the case of high lyric tenor, contralto, or mezzo-soprano voices.

Hum through first. The MAH vowel is to be kept bright. Again, the pitch may be varied slightly. Try the other vowels.

Use only one breath. Sing *pp*, *p*, *mp*, *mf*, in that order, as you gradually increase power. All vowels will then possess equal ranges of dynamic. Helped by a slow tempo and carefully executed *portamenti*, exercises 28i and 28ii further encourage Modes One to Two movement via

*momentarily* mixed mechanism. Practise strictly as indicated at this pitch (or up, or down, one semitone, depending on the comfort felt on the B3). The exercise looks (and is) appropriate for developing the mod-

ern lyric tenor, but the majority of countertenors move almost immediately into strong Mode Two, not into the permanently mixed voice condition of the modern tenor, for notes at about E4.

The full version is in the two exercises below. Be careful to allow enough breath for a loud (unforced) finish. Remember to keep *all* placements high:

The controlled *diminuendo* is more difficult. Try the Latin word *mene* (meh-neh) only when you have mastered the vowel version.

*Continue to employ portamento to all intervals for the present.* Be prepared to sound drunk! This exercise is designed to smooth the voice out, to achieve flexibility and fluency in varying the balance of the sinuses. Use it at a variety of pitches. Begin with that shown above, so that the jump of a third occurs across the 'change' area. Later, sing it to all the vowels: (i) one vowel throughout and (ii) mixed.

Use *portamento* for the change interval of a fifth. This useful exercise is to test that the Modes Two and One registers are placed high and similarly. The first (Mode Two) C4 is approached lightly, with care, to place the voice high and forward. The second C4 is sung in light, but full-toned, Mode One, keeping much the same sinus placing. The first B 3 is in Mode One, but so light as to feel like Mode Two register. The second B 3 is stronger again. Continue in this way. Use a variety of closely related pitches for the exercise, thus ensuring maximum benefit; but

**31i**



**31ii**



**31iii**



Modes One/Two exchange will need to be adjusted, for obvious reasons. Eventually, you will find it difficult to differentiate between the registers. *Portamenti* continue to be valuable for smoothing. It is not, of course, suggested that clean interval movement be banished: it is merely that from slow comes fast *portamento*; from this develops *legato*, and efficient, effective inter-register movement. Once established, the voice is ready for all demands, styles and periods of repertoire, including a return to an early-music crispness of transit, and mode of movement.

Exercises i to iii are related to no.16 and involve *amplitude* for the most part. They consist of (resultantly) a low-pitched Mode Two start, moving into a Mode One note of the same pitch, yet (resultantly) 'higher' in vocal feel. White's Technique students will find it already covered in their course, although differently explained. Other students should not be surprised if sliding one register to another on one note, or *legato* at tiny intervals, is still difficult at this stage. Concentrate on sinus placing, never on the throat. Never work this exercise for more than five minutes, but return to it once or twice a day. Try the other vowels. In time, a true *crescendo* and *diminuendo* will be possible in this change area on a single note – Mode Two to upper Mode One to full Mode One to upper Mode One to Mode Two, as above.

**32**    This is another exercise to help maintain the kind of control described in exercise 31. Take a lengthy prose text, preferably from memory, and intone on a single note (pitched perhaps $G_3$-$C_4$). Begin each sentence, or long clause, in Mode Two, *crescendo* gently into Mode One, and *diminuendo* to finish in Mode Two. Do not force the voice. Maintain all attention on the sinus cavities. Mastery of this capability will be a valuable indication of control gained, not of a technical capability to be used often – the countertenor would not need full Mode One power for his regular repertoire. When mastered, reverse the Modes One / Two directions.

**33**    As a final exercise in register negotiation, take a simple four-part hymn tune or song and sing the lower three parts as a single voice; beginning, say, in the alto, sliding into the tenor, then to bass and so on, taking advantage of the movement of the harmony to enter and leave each voice part. The result will be a wide-ranging, even voice which is versatile. Do not, of course, attempt any bass notes below $C_3$. Now repeat exercises 24–33, standing up. It must be  acknowledged that some modern choirmasters seem to dislike the full-range countertenor in ensemble and choir-stall-based solo, preferring to hear the gradual fading of Mode Two tone as it descends in pitch, rather than an equalised voice moving into its next register. Oddly, the same choirmaster will sometimes add a tenor voice to the (choral) alto at that point, thus rather defeating the object. Yet not only the choral but the solo repertoire of the historical counciltenor quite often seems to presuppose the use of the fullest possible vocal range, with its various colorations and effects. Look at later music, too, by such men as Samuel Sebastian Wesley, Edward Bairstow, and Benjamin Britten.

To conclude this section, and to underline the importance of through-range capability, even if the singer does not always choose to use it, we might consider the extensive range of the highly-trained boy chorister – often a strong low $G_3$ or even $F_3$, to perhaps $D_6$. If, in the adult alto or countertenor (of, shall we say, modest vocal gifts), the vocal range is restricted to a Mode Two register of equally modest length; the bizarre situation can arise in which the man's voice is weaker than the boy's below middle $C_3$. An alto who is out-gunned by perhaps a low single treble at similar pitch does not bode well for choral balance or for effective duets and verse work. The same goes for stage work and singing with an orchestra. Not that all specialist Mode Two countertenors are weak-toned below $C_4$ – far from it! My point is that for countertenors who are, the boy's voice production shows them the way: he uses and enjoys his full range. He does not limit himself, purposely. The child is father to the man. In this case, boy surely demonstrates to man fullest use of intrinsic vocal range. And, paradoxically, because the man is also father to the boy, it is he who (usually) teaches the boy to use voice to fullest effect and range. There is irony here, indeed.

In one way, the alto with weak low notes could be called the casualty of a particular search. I refer to the eternal quest for a 'genuine, natural, one-register voice' – i.e. for a singularly-endowed vocal student. Such a pursuit can seem, at first, like looking for the end of a rainbow, or Utopia; but this is not so: the one-register voice *very* occasionally can be located. It is, however, a rarity in any voice-type or designation. Countertenors, altos, often, it would seem, feel themselves to be this rarity. A tiny few may be correct; but for the rest, the voice is simply limited in range, by choice. In many cases, like any other vocal type about which such a claim is made, tonal strength is lacking in its lower notes.

Of course, in the case of the higher notes of the high countertenor, and indeed many sopranos, the one-register ideal tends to become forgotten as excitement ensues about extending the range upwards. That new, quasi-register changes occur is almost unnoticed, or becomes irrelevant. There is usually little or no interest in low notes, or extension in that direction. Because the high countertenor, or the light soprano, is usually determined to avoid all use of Mode One, it is axiomatic that the singer's low notes (on which the vocal range ends as it were, prematurely) lack bite or tonal strength. So, below a weak 'low end' to the voice, lie unused notes.

This need not matter when we consider the *solo* repertoire, or wherever else the personal choice of the singer is involved. Again, I underline that many high countertenors have good notes below the stave, and upwards too. Some, while weak or almost non-existent below $C_4$, possess a very impressive range indeed above it; some to high castrato-like capability. Most specialist Mode Two men gratefully use the (quasi) register changes available to them, *except* the major register change – Mode Two to Mode One. We should reflect, of course, that it is not mere range, upward, downward, or both; but what one does with one's instrument, musically, which counts. The artist is so much more than his instrument.

All that is important matter, but I finish by reiterating the importance of the lower notes in ensemble, choir (early and classical works), and a good proportion of the early and classical solo countertenor repertoire. He who wishes to be heard must be strong in the lower half of his vocal range. The countertenor is concerned, first and foremost, with the *alto* area of the musical spectrum. All the artistry in the universe is wasted, except to its originator, if it cannot be heard.

# The exclusive use of Mode Two, and further development of the through-range

'High' countertenors, having at least examined the foregoing section, should now re-enter the course in a practical way. The following figures are to stretch further and equalize the head area downwards as well as (later) upwards in pitch. 'Low' countertenors, fresh from exercises 24–31, may wish to leave 34 until after 38ii; but otherwise should now attempt to incorporate the experiences recently gained. They should, however, sing all [H] (therefore [MT]) exercises too. Certain exercises are provided with alternative pitch.

(Henceforth, work all exercises sitting, then standing.) Begin slowly, breaking and breathing not only at all double bar-lines but, when needed, at the indications. Work to eradicate these extra points as you increase speed. Do not force the lower notes. Concentrate on a broader, not louder, tone as the pitch descends and the sphenoidal cavities* are

*For low countertenors, that is, who employ Mode One.

engaged increasingly. Volume will develop. Low countertenors should begin exercise 34 *gently and very slowly*, especially over the register changes. Remember that Mode One notes should be resonated in the skull cavities, like those of Mode Two. When exercise 34 has become mastered, transpose it up: a semitone at a time, until the top note is perhaps $D\sharp 4$ or $E4$, according to what feels comfortable.

**35**    *This, and following exercises involving heavy accents, should first be worked omitting them.*

Exercise 35 is a good daily exercise. Make all notes equal and distinct. Sing the top note firmly but do not strain. Watch intonation. Use moderately fast speed, and one breath only.

**36**

Sing this very smoothly, with dignity. Expand strongly on the accented $G\sharp 4$. Try for as much expression as possible. Breathe only as marked. Do this exercise two or three times only: it can be tiring. Vary the key within *comfortable* range.

**37**

Work exercise 37 reversing the dynamics after mastering it as shown.

**38i**

Begin work in B major if found preferable.

Use identical dynamics and vowels in both i. and ii.

**38ii**

Use *crescendo* and *diminuendo* identically in 38i and 38ii. Later, try reversing the dynamics. Only use the stresses gently to begin with. Sing in strict time. Make the four ritard notes especially firm. Breath is to be taken only at the crotchet rest.

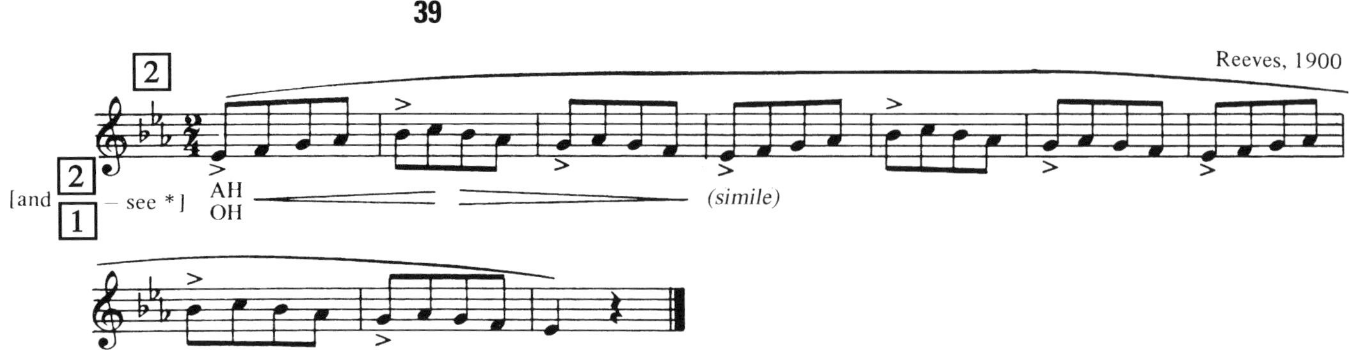


Use AH or OH throughout. As a change, the middle phrase may be sung *mezza voce*, the first and last phrases in fuller voice. Sing the exercise in one breath.

*'Through-voice'(i.e. Mode Two/Mode One) countertenors should sing it both at pitch, and down perhaps a seventh, in D major. Vary it by reversing dynamics.

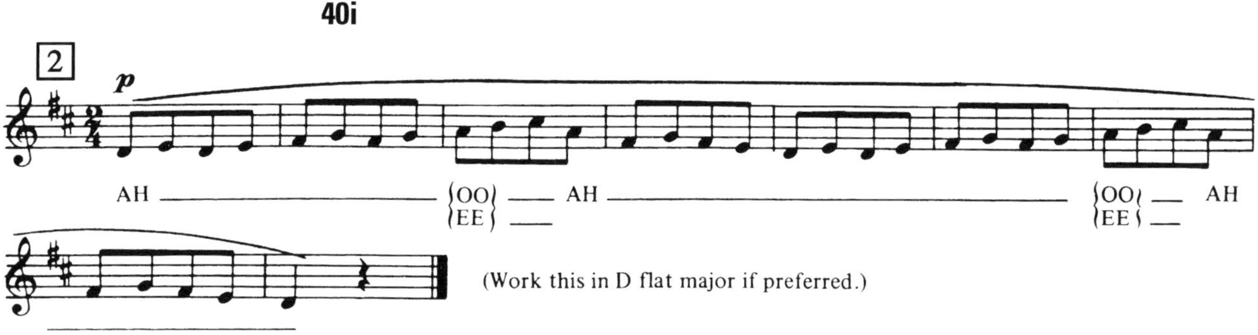


Exercise 40i will help to strengthen lower Mode Two, and encourage development of the 'small', or 'pipe' register at the top end of Mode Two, referred to in Section E. Make the OO and EE soft and clear. Begin work at *piano* volume throughout. Later, sing the AH passes up to *forte*.

Version ii will continue to encourage the uniting of Modes Two and One.

Use 41 throughout your comfortable range. Sing moderately quickly, but in strict time, and tuning the exact intervals between notes. Increase speed as you improve. Alter the exercise by accenting the upper notes. Do not attempt too rapid a speed if you employ a register change. It is probably too early to expect anything more than ♪ = 192.

Exercises 42i and 42ii are for firm, unforced note initiation. Concentrate on the frontal sinuses, as if, for a split second, the note begins there in advance of anywhere else.* Work *mp*, then *mf* throughout.

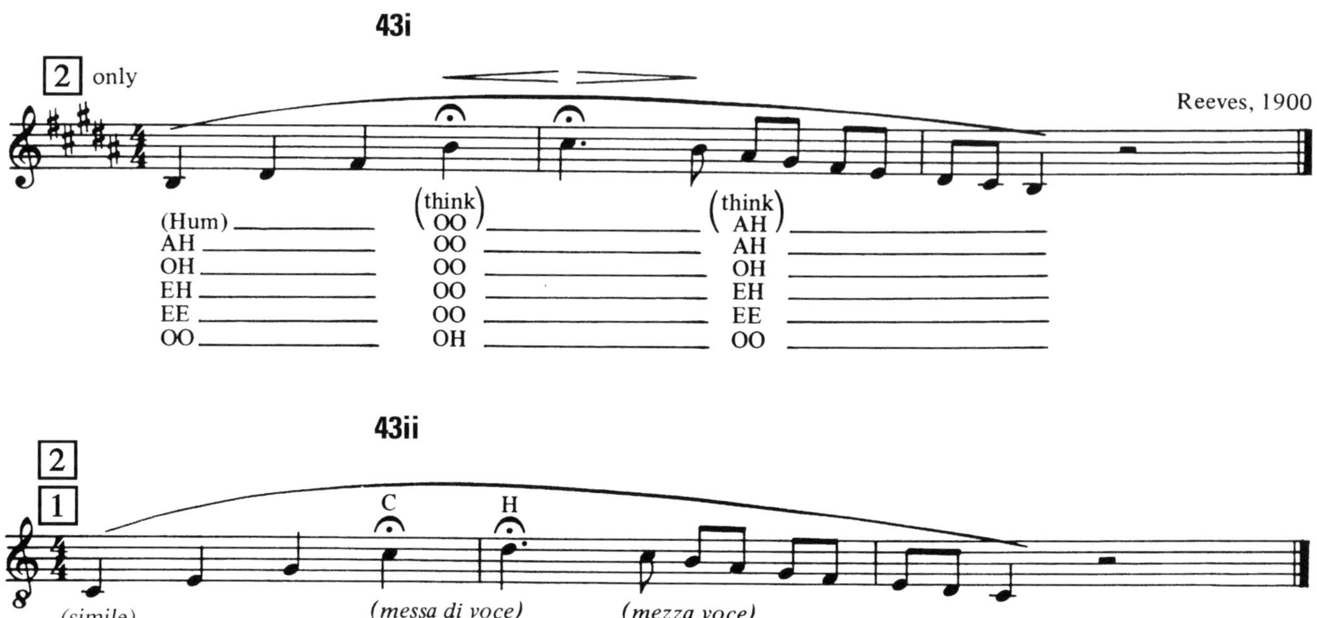


Exercise 43i is useful for practising lower Mode Two to upper, thinned. (Use also in conjunction with 'small' or 'pipe' register, later.) For low countertenors, it is helpful to develop and further smooth the Mode One-to-Mode Two transition (43ii). For this purpose it may be taken in B major, as at (43i). Sing the *arpeggio* firmly, medium speed. Swell the voice on the high paused notes (slight *messa di voce*), then die away quickly into *mezza voce*, and remain so for the scale, unhurried and clear. Engage differing vowels as shown. Use this exercise only a few times in succession. Even when done correctly, it can be tiring. *(Messa di voce* means *crescendo* and *diminuendo* on a long note. *Mezza voce* indicates only moderate volume of tone: half voice.)

---

* Only when you have completed this course, sing a phrase with one word per note, in front of a looking glass.

Repeat over and over. Observe the mouth movements closely. They will appear fractionally behind the sounds

produced, and they are.

Exercises 44 i and ii are good daily exercises. Sing exact intervals and do not use *portamento* but true *legato*. Use only the middle of the voice: reasonable power or *mezza voce*: *moderato* to *allegro*. Sing 44ii in one breath to the same vowel as 44i.

### The English primary and most important secondary vowels

Ours is very much a language of diphthongs. The purity of Italian is not equalled, but there is an incredible range of subtleties and versatilities in English – now arguably the world language. I have adopted Charles Cleall's excellent system of representing English vowels visually: capitals for long vowels, and underlined lower-case for short ones, using a key sentence. Under it I have placed symbols from the International Phonetic Alphabet.*

1. OO  <u>oo</u>  OH AW <u>o</u> AH   <u>u</u> ER <u>a</u>   e   AY  I   <u>i</u> EE       (Cleall)

2. You should go for top marks, son. Perhaps then they might in-crease     (*Standard English pronunciation.*)

3. u.    u   o ɔ: ɔ   a   ʌ  ə: æ   *e*   e   aɪ   I   i       (IPA)

---

*This seems to be essential to help students not readily familiar with standard-southern or *received*-English

pronunciation. I give these symbols once only: students needing them must relate them to the Cleall system as

they go. See the Booklist.

This sentence, said slowly, getting the vowels as true as possible, and pronouncing them as though the syllables were stressed, gives the tonal quality which is intended to be represented by the capitals and italics. Try singing it slowly on a monotone.

45i

45ii

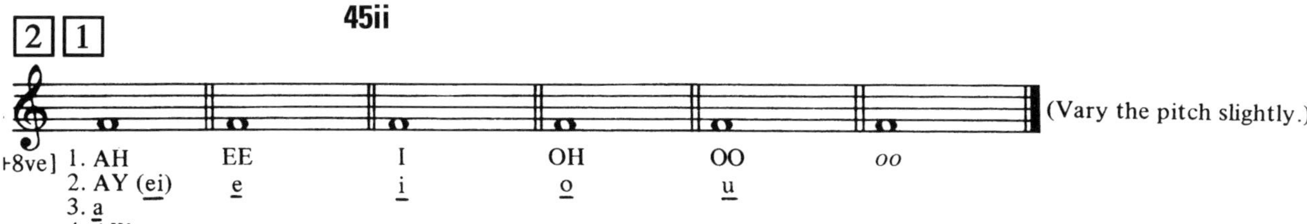



The student is urged to persevere till the English vowels are correctly sounded. Because three of the five primary vowels are themselves diphthongs, it is advisable to examine the English diphthongs on this page. Do not confuse the pronunciation of English and Italian vowels. OH, for example, denotes different sounds in each.

46i

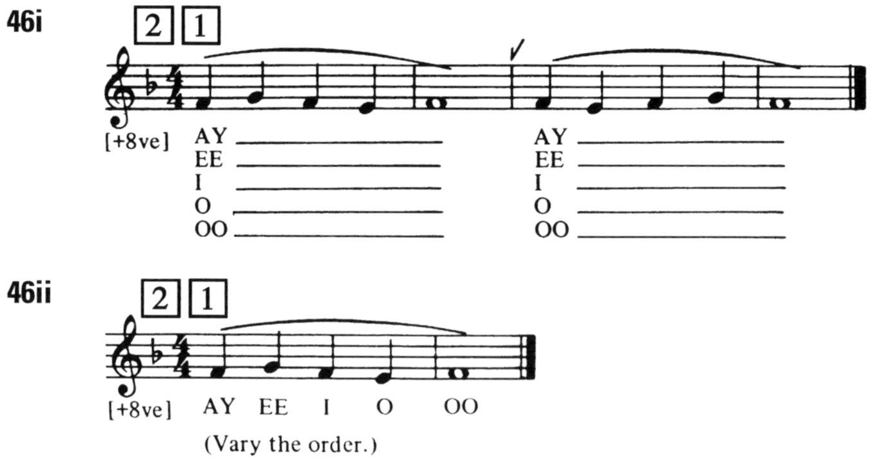



46ii



Follow the above five vowels with the others shown in exercise 44, fitting them to the musical phrase.

**46iii**   Now use the main English vowels to exercise 16 (AH–AY–AH), 17–23, and all subsequent numbers in which Italian vowels have been used.

**English vowels and diphthongs (see analysis in Cleall, pages 21-22).**

AY ($\underline{e}^i$)   OY(AW$^i$)   I   (I$^i$)   WE ($^{OO}$E, almost $^{OO}$i/$^{OO}$EE)
OH (OH$^{OO}$)*   OW (AH$^{OO}$)   (AH$^i$)   letter U ($^i$OO)

**46iv**

(Vary the order.)

**47**   Use and freely adapt the following phrases to exercise 46, then return to exercise 11 in all its variants:

(i) (O) no John, no John, no. (etc.)

(ii) Many, many men. (etc.)

(iii) Why O why O why? (etc.)

(iv) Ding a dong a ding.  (etc.)

(v)  Penny penny bun. (etc.)

(vi ) May I sway away. (etc.)

(vii) Roam slowly o'er the lea with me. (etc.)

(viii) Oh you are a mucky kid. (etc.)

---

*Be careful not to pronounce this as EH$^{OO}$.  Better to approach it in similar manner to the Italian OH (hot), then adjust slightly.

### Some pronunciations which can be difficult for the singer

**48i**

These sounds, short when speaking, are often prolonged when singing. Vary the passage in pitch by a tone or two, up and down.

**48ii**

These diphthongs must be negotiated carefully; make the second sound short but clear (*). Ask someone to identify each as you sing it. You may be surprised!

**48iii**

(Finalise the last 'er' or 'w' very quickly, at *. For more work with compound vowels, see Cleall, page 22, and Kennedy Scott, pages 134–139.)

**Pronunciations easily confused by the singer, and useful for practice**

**49i**
Poor, Paw, Pore                    Soar, Saw, Sore, Sower
Moor, Maw, More, Mower             Violet, Varlet, Volute
Mourn, Morn                        Tour, Tor, Too

Place the O and L at the very end of the minim (*). Use the phrase as indicated for each family.

**49ii**

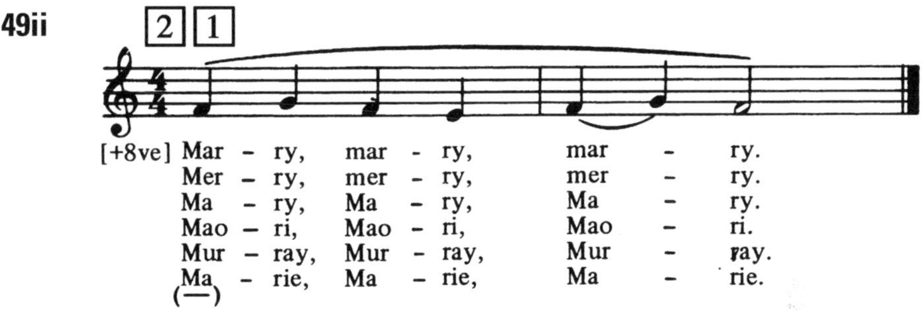


**49iii**    Adapt this phrase to the music:
Marry merry Maori, Mary Marie Murray.


Exercise 49 needs care. When you have mastered the differences, alternate the words freely in their family groups. Ask a listener to identify each word.

**Chromatic intonation (this may be done after exercise 52)**

**50**

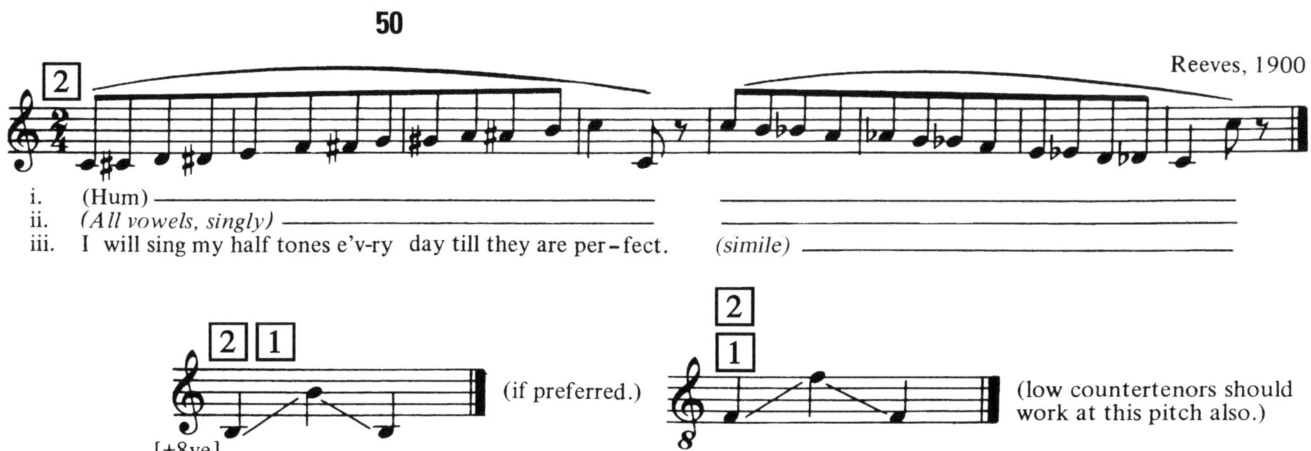


This is a useful exercise both for tuning and enunciation, and is to be sung moderately quickly, the words distinct but *legato* as in ordinary speech. Do not jerk or force the octave leap to finish. When you have mastered the pitches shown, work in any which are comfortable.

**The vowel scale (based on English vowels, but incorporating the Italian)**

This is based on the phenomenon that vowels possess inherent pitch. The vowel scale proceeds from low to high in that order: OO, OH (English), AH, AY, I (lie), EE, so that as a result, acoustically, the highest tones will be produced most readily when singing the vowels in the order just given. Try the following, which includes both long and short English vowels:

**51i**    Whisper: OO oo OH AW o AH  u ER  a   e AY I  i  EE
(book)        (top)    (cut)   (cat) (then)   (in)

**51ii**

A slight sensation of rising pitch will be felt from OO to AY, then reversed to OO. After trying the full version, as in 51i, on the monotone, explore the sensations of the following:

Sing it softly, striking each note clearly and distinctly, taking a slight breath after each. Take full breath only at the start. Vary the key of the *arpeggio* and use Mode One and Mode Two where appropriate. Re-study and re-work previous exercises in the fresh light of the vowel scale. For detailed examination of this, see Berton Coffin's *Overtones of Bel Canto* (see Booklist). The vowel scale helps the student train himself to watch for faulty intonation.

## A few words about consonants

Comparatively little has been said so far  on this subject. All too often, the student or inexperienced singer treats consonants as tight or explosive interruptions to the singing tone. English singers, for example, particularly in choirs, frequently confuse the D with the T, rendering the word DEED as TEET. Some consonants should be sung on (voiced) and D is one of them. Here are a few pointers to the pronunciation of the main consonants:

| *Voiced (sonants)* | *Unvoiced (surds)* |
|---|---|
| D, V, L, M, N, R, Z, B, G, W, Y | T, F, K, P, S, H |

Voiced consonants must never over-tighten, but should be almost *bounced*, particularly the R (roll it*), and B, D, G. Thus the word DEED should always be practised Dee-Duh, gradually shortening the second half. But in order to carry to an audience, unvoiced consonants, like T,

---

* Unless subtlety, not clarity, is the main object in any particular performance context; or unless the demands

of another language dictate otherwise (a principle generally applicable).

often need an element of mix in them. Thus the word TAINT is approached as T(d)AINT(d). In other cases:

F often needs a little V in it
K often needs a little G in it (as in *game*)
P often needs a little  B in it
S often needs a little Z in it

Consonants may further be divided into explodents, sibilants, vocals and aspirates. Kennedy Scott deals with the whole subject at much greater length and in microscopic detail, exceeding what we need here; but I shall give one more example of don't. Never allow yourself to convert T (our old problem consonant) into S: explodent into sibilant. This is a common fault, and renders TIGER as T(s)IGER, or even TSIGER. As a final comment, remember that no consonant must be allowed to tighten the musculature of jaws and mouth, with effect resembling more *rigor* than vigour, so that the vocal tone itself becomes tight and inhibited. The jaw action must remain easy and without stress. Absolute clarity of enunciation during singing need not, and must not, result in the interruption and destruction of the vocal line.

## Mood, expression and more agility

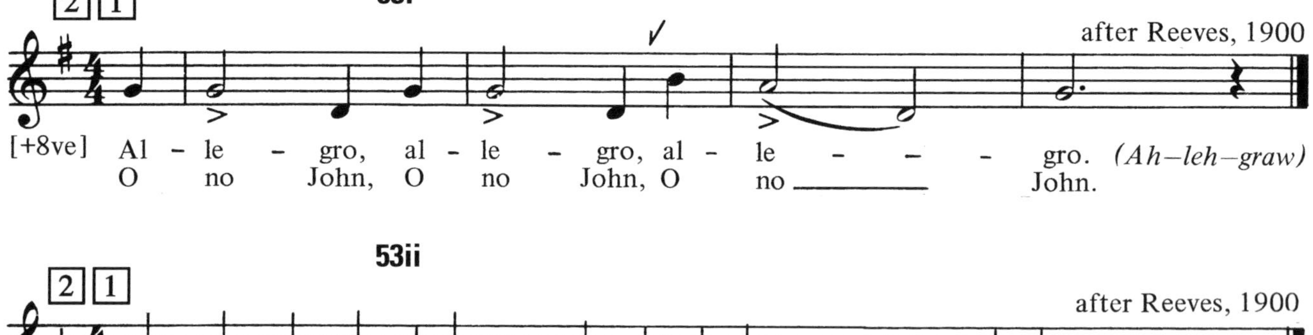


In these exercises, use different tone colours for happy, sad, thoughtful, angry, etc., and use greatly varying speed and volume.

Use these versions after mastering and exploiting 53i and 53ii.

*Include exercise 54 only if you have a comfortable top E.* Alternatively, try it down, beginning on an F or E. This passage demonstrates well the use of violin-string-like tonal qualities, available over the voice range – each area possessing its own colour. Note the composer's awareness of the vowel scale. The top note should always be carefully controlled, thin and not over-loud'; certainly not pushed.

Try exercise 55 also a semitone down, and at various pitches upwards.

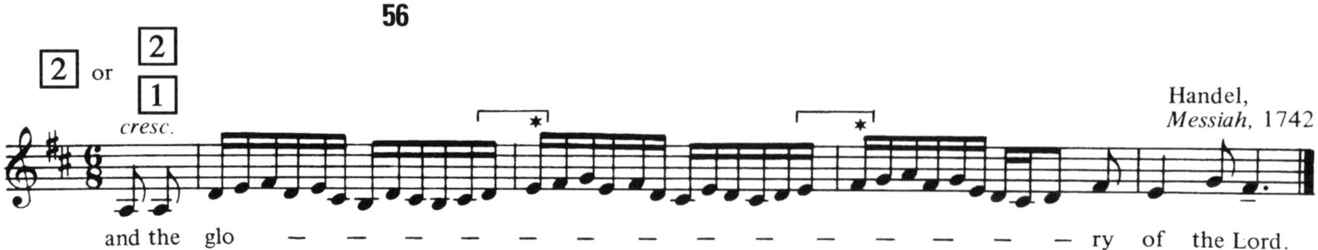


Practise the above run as follows. Put a stress on the notes marked *; stop, breathe, then begin the next section on the note immediately preceding it. Eliminate breathing point no.1 first. At the final stage, you should be able to control the run using gradual *crescendo*. Make a conscious choice of either *legato* or slightly detached style, having mastered both. The exercise may be practised in a variety of keys for versatility; but expertise, above all, must be secured at the printed pitch, and one semitone down – which is widely considered to approach Handel's pitch in England, and Germany, at least.

# Exercises of greater length

These studies could be worked at in parallel with the Vaccai musical course recommended in the Booklist. It is suggested that, in addition, low countertenors obtain the tenor-pitch version listed there, and that all students begin with Vaccai's lessons I–II, then return to my exercise 56. Follow this with Vaccai up to and including lesson V, after which work on my exercise 57. Low countertenors are recommended to work each Vaccai exercise in tenor and alto pitch, in that order, but watching never to force Mode One beyond its established bounds.

**57**

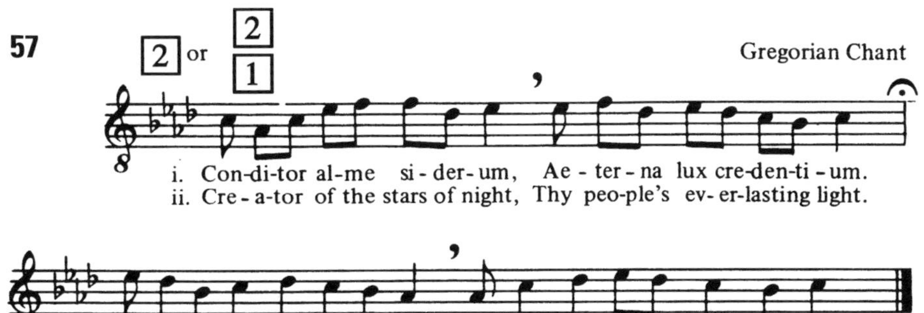


also at:

Sing the above with *legato* phrasing and in strict time, both texts, one after the other. Choose a slow speed to start with. Apply this also to the following exercise: i, ii, iii, in prompt succession.

**58**

Exercise 58 is for both low and high countertenors. The latter should not sing the bracketed passages up an octave, or perform as if they consider the exercise a low one. With such a text, they should not strive for so much volume, low down, that they sound *grim*. A light, airy use of Mode Two will express the mood perfectly. Concentrate on achieving the optimum brightness from correct use of the cavities, with a major part being played by the frontal sinuses. The volume may not be great, but the tone will tell enough with light accompaniment. Volume will, in any case, develop slowly and imperceptibly with vocal usage.

Exercises 59–61, extensive in length, are from the late 17th and early 18th centuries. It will be seen that two are from modern editions, with the countertenor part shown as for tenor, while the third is reproduced from its original printing, in which, of course, the alto clef is employed.

There are those who maintain that the character, employment, and even existence of the countertenor voice, as we know it, depends largely on the question of historical pitch. The argument often appears to be that because employment of a lower pitch seems automatically to restore countertenor parts, in some cases, to the range of the lyric tenor, then all countertenors were simply like modern lyric tenors. We have examined and discounted the latter possibility, earlier in this book; but it cannot be denied that pitch is a vexed question. It seems fashionable, at the moment, to perform *all* 17th-century secular works down a full semitone from our modern $A_4 = 440$, whatever the country of origin, despite clear indications that pitch varied much, even within each country, well into the 18th century and beyond. There appears to have been at least three main pitches in operation in England in the late 17th century, one of which seems to have been about $A_4=440$. Another was nearly, but not quite, a semitone below this; yet another lay about a tone higher than $A_4=440$.

Academics argue on; some musical directors now employ modern-style lyric tenors rather than countertenors of any variety. The countertenor, meanwhile, must avoid aiding the spread of heresy, error, and his own neglect by not being feeble in any vocal department!

The student is advised to study the exercises at the pitch shown, but also to try them using alternative pitches as indicated above. Bracketed sections would have to be adjusted accordingly. It must be admitted that many high countertenors will find sufficient volume difficult with some low countertenor parts, now made lower by the drop of a semitone or so; but then, most totally Mode Two men would not, it would seem, have expected to sing these parts in any but the most intimate chamber performance.

Exercise 59 should be worked alone till mastered, then perhaps a *suitable*, sympathetic tenor and bass might be persuaded to join in *gently*, to help gauge balance and effectiveness. Passages under the indication are to be sung in Mode One. The work is really for the low countertenor, but high countertenors should use it for practice, retaining Mode One voice for the whole exercise, however *piano* they may have to sing the lowest notes. Ultra-high voices could omit the bars which are bracketed or, perhaps for the sake of practice, sing the passages up an octave (not normally to be done in performance). Begin now to bring out the dramatic qualities in exercises which offer scope for this. Suggested breathing is indicated by ∕ .

**59**  *Extract from Purcell's 'O, I'm Sick of Life'*

# O, I'M SICK OF LIFE

Realized by Arnold Goldsbrough

air: what should thy wrath in - cense To pun-ish him who knows not his of-fence? Ah!__
air.
air.
(Counter tenor)
__ dost thou in op-pres-sion take de- light? Wilt thou thy ser-vant fold_______ in__ shades of
night And smile__ on wick-ed coun-sels? Dost thou see With eyes of flesh? Is truth con -

**60**    *Extract from Purcell's 'The Fairy Queen' (1692)*

*In some versions: Xsansi.

___your eyes have made   Yes, made.   She that in love makes
least de-fence   Wounds ___________ ev - er   with the sur - est dart,
Beau-ty may cap - - ti-vate the sense,   But kind - ness,   but ___
kind - ness on - ly gains the heart.   She   heart.

### The C clef

Mention must be made of this, and examples given in it. Early music uses it extensively for alto and tenor, respectively, and today's countertenors and tenors must be able to sing from it when required to do so. I discuss the matter in my book *The History and Technique of the Counter-Tenor*; but let us say here that though C clef is not much liked by singers today, the advantages of it are that it usually places the voice part squarely into the stave, instead of half hanging below, using leger lines. Visual and mental considerations can affect tone colour. To illustrate this simply, consider the following passage, using the C clef in its alto position, followed by the modern G clef:

It would seem possible that the basis for some of the modern tenor's claim to the lower countertenor repertoire rests on the *look* of the part when in its original C clef. Today's tenor sees there an apparent *tenor* part, admittedly a high or extremely high one. In familiar, modern usage, it is merely a tone out in appearance, compared to a normal tenor part shown in G clef. In addition, the use of C clef for both alto and tenor parts – although on different lines of the stave – underlines, quite rightly, the original relationship of alto to tenor. But as we have seen, the early tenor used a different technique to that of his modern counterpart.

Add to these considerations the later adoption of treble clefs and many low leger lines for alto parts, and the scene is set – not only for the development of a practical vocal gulf, but an academic arena fecund for papers earnest and published discourses intense!

Yet the matter is so very simple in essence. *The countertenor is a high voice, not a low one, even in its lowest reaches.* Mental image is very important and I repeat this advisedly. We should use the C clef much more than now we do, though it must be admitted that reading from one today is not as easy and familiar as once it was. We are used to a full vocal score, and taking leads from other parts or the accompaniment. The dedicated, specialist early-music singer, though, must work from original editions and manuscripts with familiarity and panache. The more general countertenor singer should work conscientiously from alto clef as regularly as possible in order to benefit from the therapeutic advantages which it bestows.

**61**  (See the Marcello example on the next page)

Do not allow yourself to sing from the top line of the keyboard reduction with the intention of avoiding the alto clef! Persevere, and keep strictly to your own vocal line.

*NOTE*

The student should have worked through Sections A–C of the course before attempting Sections D and E. It is vital that this be so, for the method has been planned strictly to proceed in careful order, particularly in the case of a student working without a suitable teacher. It should be re-stated that the approach used here is essentially subjective and uses, generally, language of one singer to another. Nothing of the following technical matter must be allowed to interfere with the fundamental approach used so far – which is that of MENTAL IMAGE, and its practical flowering and beneficial results.

**61**

**Extract from Psalm 16, by Marcello (1686 - 1739)**

Having experienced and explored the workings of the voice first-hand, we shall now sum up the register areas visually: areas which for the most part have been negotiated already. Much of the following laryngeal information and detail on muscular matters should be considered strictly *supplementary* to the act of singing. For reasons given in the Preface, I hesitate to supply excessive theory and physiological matter in a manual that sets out to help develop an historical voice. But this is a written version: a book, not a practical demonstration; and it is for the teacher too. He/she will need the maximum information for obvious reasons. Also, as I have stated, the countertenor still needs to justify his technique and *raison d'être* occasionally! However, consciousness of fold action should not be allowed to intrude whilst singing. The student must be strict with himself on this. Read and digest these matters, then put them at the back of the memory.

Apparently to clarify registers, but really to demonstrate the contradictory world of singing theory and pedagogic matters vocal, on the following page is a related list comprising most of the nomenclature variously employed by teachers, singers, and in singing treatises. Each column shows alternative terms used variously by writers and theorists. Those employed chiefly in the present work are in capitals and/or bold. Remember that columns one and two denote their straightforward conditions, *not their mixed state*, for high tenor notes. There would be inevitable disagreement about column 2 from certain quarters. Indeed, it is certain that, like much in the world of vocal pedagogy, the configuration of this table could in itself be contentious. Equally, together with Figure 6 on pages 90–91, it not only best illustrates my thesis, but should be most helpful for the countertenor.

| Mode One | Mode Two<br>*(Lower)* | Mode Two<br>*(Higher)* | Mode Two<br>*(Highest)* |
|---|---|---|---|
| | | | Small voice/register |
| 'Chest' register    HIGHER<br>LOWER | 'Head' register    LOWER | 'Head' register    UPPER | 'Head' register |
| **Basic** register/voice | | | |
| **Mainly sphenoidal sinus** | **Mainly ethmoidal sinus** | **Mainly frontal sinus** | **Pure frontal sinus** |
| **Fundamental** | | | **Pipe** |
| Lower register | Upper register | Falsetto | Falsettissimo |
| Thick voice UPPER / LOWER | Thin voice LOWER | Thin voice UPPER | Flute |
| Pulse | Modal | Loft | Small bore |
| Mode | Pharyngeal voice  register | Super falsetto | Whistle register |
| Natural voice | Middle falsetto | Upper falsetto | Dimple falsetto |
| Full voice | Medium register | Fine register | Bird voice |
| Long reed | Throat voice | Mode 3 | Mode 4 |
| | Narrowed voice | | Bell register |
| | 'Witch' voice | | |
| | Marginal voice | | |
| | Short reed | | |
| | Mode 2 | | |

**Table 1**  The register jungle.

Reading from left to right, columns 1 to 4 illustrate the near impossibility for agreement on the subject of registers in the world of singing. Titles in bold or capitals denote significant use in this work.

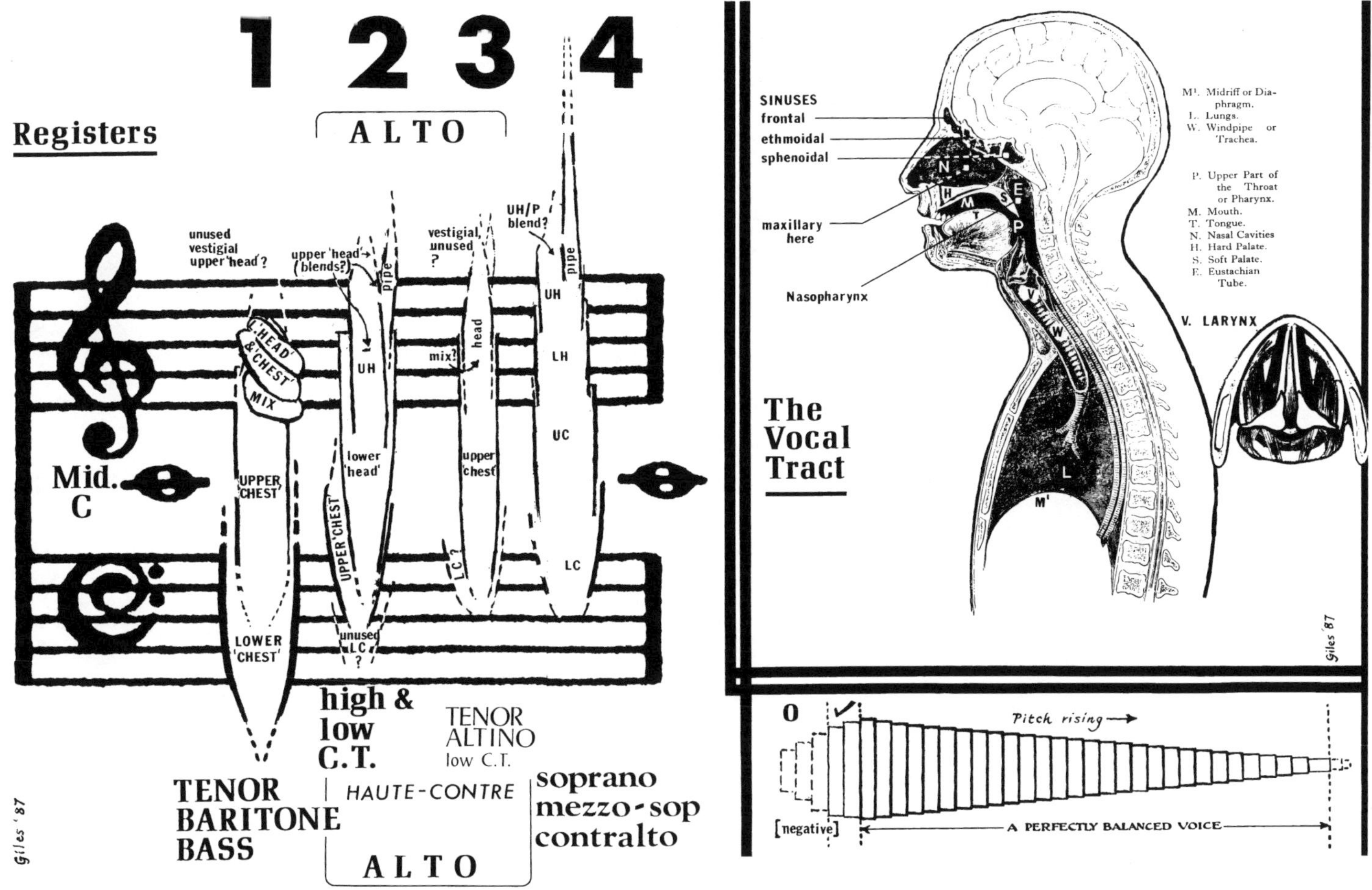


THE CONVENTIONAL VIEW

A general guide to male and female registration shown compositely, including the counter-tenor types. Notice the ranges and overlapping, but remember that individual voices may possess slight variations. The author has met and heard more than one singer who could demonstrate totally convincing ability, with genuine and beautiful timbre, throughout all the male-voice ranges shown here. Though such powers are something of a rarity, the human voice is a miracle of versatility and adaptability.

EQUALISATION

This, discounting dramatic and expressive demands, is the historical, pre-Romantic period ideal. In reality, the working singer, solo or in ensemble, is often dictated to by circumstances, musical and otherwise, to attempt notes beyond his or her effective range in this regard.

As the diagram suggests, high notes thus attempted should sound merely smaller, tonally, if the technique is correct. This preserves equalisation. It can be seen, however, that progressively more feeble low notes spoils it. Exceptional artistry can often nullify certain aspects of this; and there are, of course, occasions when soft low notes and loud high ones are entirely appropriate.

**Figure 5**  Registers, vocal tract and equalisation.

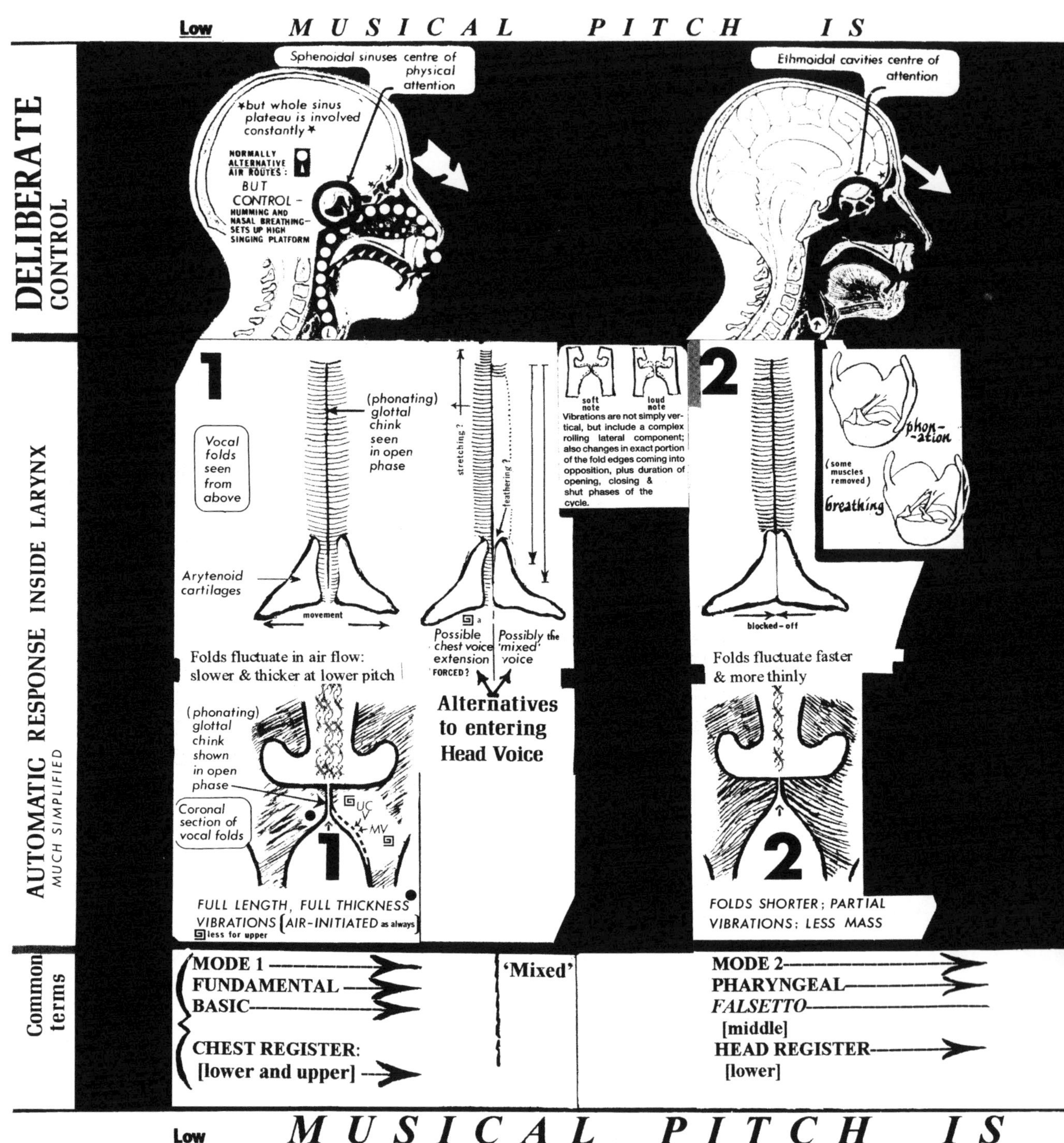


**Figure 6**  Control, laryngeal response and registers.

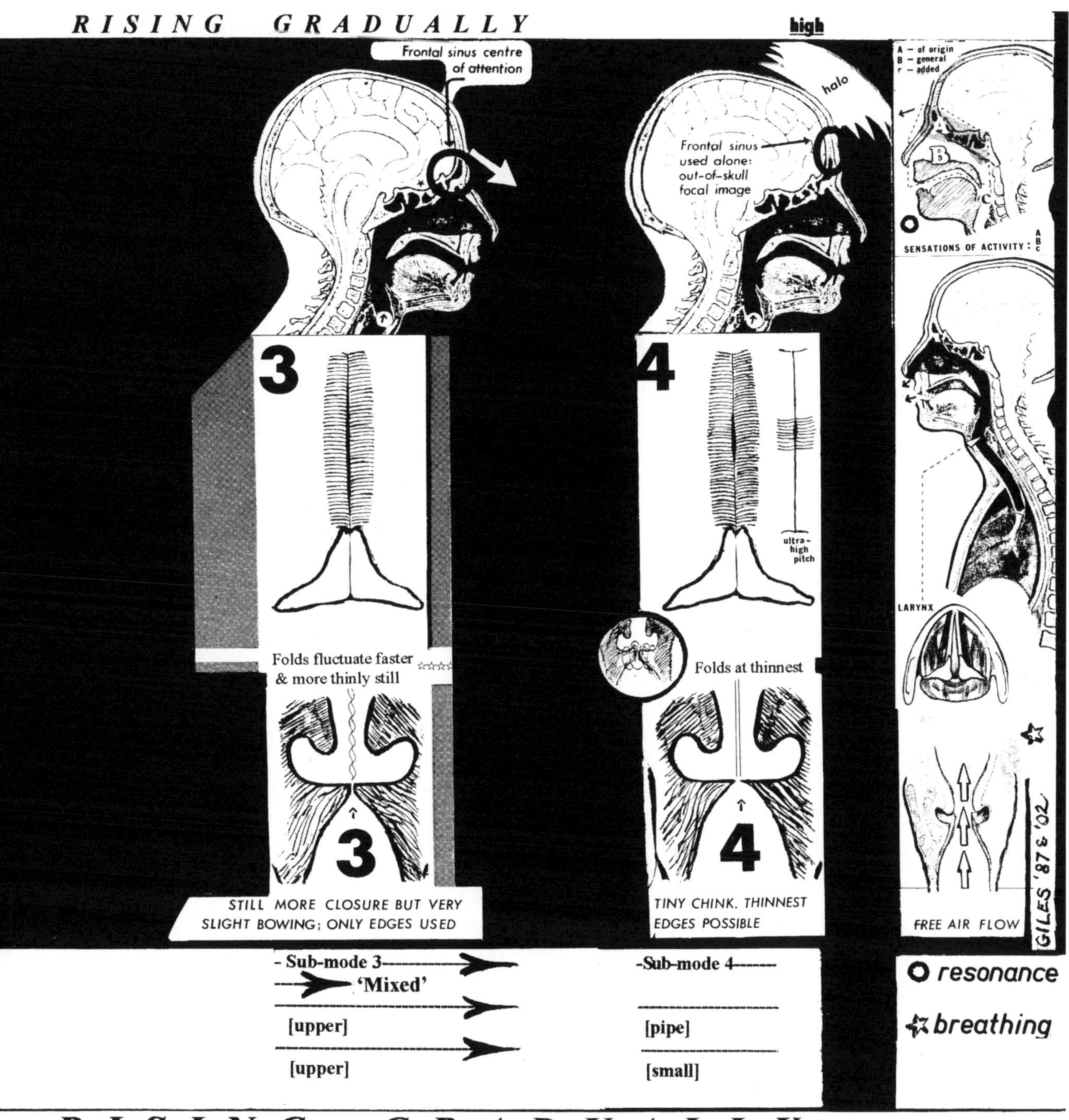
RISING GRADUALLY
high
Frontal sinus centre of attention
halo
Frontal sinus used alone: out-of-skull focal image
A — of origin
B — general
r — added
SENSATIONS OF ACTIVITY:
3
Folds fluctuate faster & more thinly still
4
ultra-high pitch
Folds at thinnest
3
STILL MORE CLOSURE BUT VERY SLIGHT BOWING; ONLY EDGES USED
4
TINY CHINK. THINNEST EDGES POSSIBLE
LARYNX
GILES '87 & '02
FREE AIR FLOW
- Sub-mode 3
'Mixed'
[upper]
[upper]
-Sub-mode 4-
[pipe]
[small]
resonance
breathing

So far, the student has not been encouraged to sing very high notes. Except for the option of exercise 54, few exercises take him beyond B4 or C4. This is because the main alto repertoire and range is below this level, and because there is a natural quasi-register change which takes place at about B4. It is not such a major change as that situated about one octave below, for most countertenors; and many singers hardly know it exists. While a seamless voice is to large extent the goal of all singers, unawareness of a register-change can also allow the singer to miss a valuable added effect and tonal colour.

Though so far we have discouraged much higher vocal exploration, we have allowed the student to extend upwards slightly and occasionally. Once above B4 or so, no doubt he has mixed instinctively the upper Mode Two quality – the more disembodied sensation – with strong lower Mode Two timbre, thus combining tonal strength with higher, lighter capabilities. In Section E, exercises are provided to help separate this mix for special use and effect.

All voice-ranges share the same basic mechanisms, but their uses and the techniques of singers can vary. The larynx is situated in the trachea in the immediate path of air from the lungs. During phonation, the vocal folds, loosely closed in this airflow, become vibrated: pulsations whose miniature quality varies according to the nature of fold and flow of air. In order that the sound may be audible, the resonating chambers into vocal tone must transform the vibrations. These are the pharynx, mouth and cranial sinus cavities. Imagine an old-fashioned gramophone needle held to the record by the fingers. The sound is negligible. Connect the needle with first its diaphragm unit and tone arm, then its resonating cavities and horn, and you have a rough analogy with the voice. (The diaphragm is not, of course, analogous to the diaphragm of the human body; nor is the mouth too directly analogous to the horn.) We have already discovered and experienced the practical results of all this in our work so far. Because we have found or 'placed' the voice by now, it is perhaps all right to examine these matters, but under no circumstances should this impinge on the mental images already formed during singing,

If you can whistle at above average standard, stand before a mirror and whistle an extended *arpeggio* from one extreme to the other. Observe the mouth changes, and monitor those taking place within. We have a rough analogy to vocal fold movement, but only a rough one.

To allow pitch to ascend, more and more of the mass of the vocal folds is stretched and pulled away automatically, till the only method of achieving higher notes is for the folds to be made shorter (in one way, and one way only, like stopping a violin string, for vocal fold movement is *automatic*, and involves the passage of air). In conjunction with this shortening, initially by the arytenoid cartilages, merely the edges of the folds are engaged by now (in well-trained voices). This produces Mode Two in direct-feeling association with the frontal and ethmoidal sinuses as resonators. Further fold closure results in small register or pipe voice, using only the frontal sinus.

There is still disagreement about vocal fold-lengths as related to the usual tenor voice. Some writers insist that they are longer, and thinner than those of baritones and basses – hence the higher note capability through attenuation. Other authorities explain that the folds are shorter than for the heavier voices, and that they resemble the length of those which produce the lower voices of women. This gives them a similar pitch. The truth may be that elements of both descriptions apply to some extent to some lyric tenors. To achieve the usual tenor or baritone mixed voice, the arytenoid cartilages are almost certainly less closed – hence *partial* vibration is allowed, which results in both Modes Two and One being combined for use together on the same note. Thus we have a *spliced* or mixed upper register.

The countertenor, of course, does not normally use this mixed register, except perhaps briefly at the change point if he employs a through-voice technique. Instead of the tenor's *splice*, for the low countertenor there is a shallow *dovetailing*, the tiny overlap being the equivalent of the splice. Yet all countertenors do use a mix technique, even though it may only be lower Mode Two with upper Mode Two, plus small-register elements. The mix will usually come in at about B4, automatically, unless purposely avoided (see Section E) but many singers mix it earlier. The rare *tenor altino* type would seem to possess folds of light, almost female light, size and character, and he uses either the unmixed lower Mode Two voice above his extremely light Mode One, or a mixed register similarly to the ordinary tenor. The sound produced by the second option would differ from the usual tenor, though, because of the *tenor altino*'s unusually thinner, stretchier, small vocal folds; and it often seems to resemble the light mezzo-soprano in timbre.

The human larynx, indeed the whole vocal instrument, is certainly a miracle of adaptability and versatility. Its subtleties make even the most sophisticated musical instrument seem crude. Remember that the movements of the larynx produce no easily discernible sound in themselves. It is the resonance which the audience hears. Hence our complete attention during voice production must be far higher, on the resonating chambers, freeing the larynx to do its job naturally.

Because the singer's first concern, always, is surely how best to produce a satisfactory sound, his aural standpoint is quite properly subjective. An excellent mental image is therefore essential and creative. The various resonation chambers should be thought of, by the singer, as being engaged, note by note, almost like a rank of organ pipes, according to the *pitch* of that note; and organ stops, according to the *character* of the note. Thus, for Mode One, the sphenoidal sinus should be imagined as the source of sound, plus an element of ethmoidal cells and (small) frontal sinus, plus resonation from the pharynx and (possibly) sympathetic areas round the upper sternum (breast bone). For lower Mode Two, the main resonance should be visualised as emanating from the ethmoidal cells, plus, increasingly, the frontal sinus as the pitch rises. Think of upper Mode Two as almost completely frontal sinus in origin, plus elements of ethmoidal and pharyngeal resonance.

So all voice production should be thought of as emanating from a highly-placed system of cranial cavities. Ernest George White demonstrated that the cranial sinus-system could vary from one skull to another in size, proportion, shape and extent. Anthony W Halfhide, the E.N.T. consultant, has suggested that the frontal sinuses can be thought of, on average, as being of the size of hazel nuts; the ethmoidal and sphenoidal sinuses, of peas; and the maxillary sinuses, of walnuts: a helpful image. Charles Cleall (in a lecture to The Ernest George White Society on 11th October 1986) drew attention to the fact that, in some skulls, the sinuses are connected more than even White supposed; so that the frontal sinuses may drain into the infundibulum, and it and the ethmoidal cells into the hiatus semilunaris, and it into the maxillary sinuses, in a continuous path. Thus, a concept which some found difficult to accept becomes easier to understand, and methodology based on it not only worth using but essential to the optimum production of voice.

So we who seek to use both concept and method can be confident that attention focused on the cranial sinus system during voice production not only can never be unwise (something which few, if any, could claim about preoccupation with the larynx), but indeed is also imperative. Because the wise voice-user, singer or actor, is concentrating on production from a high point, and never on the larynx or glottis, there is no likelihood of unnatural stress building up in that larynx, This is not, of course, to advocate floppy, weak or gassy tone caused by air-loss through a loose and inefficient glottal chink. It is simply that the larynx will move naturally and efficiently if all attention is drawn away from it to the resonance cavities and focal placing. The runner thinks of his strategy, perhaps his breathing, of the tape ahead, but not of his muscular action while running.

**62i**  To underline the unique, smooth versatility and sophistication of the vocal systems, and prepare you for the next section, here is the 'wind in the chimney' exercise. Hum the deepest note in your range (low countertenors will start in low Mode One, high countertenors at the deepest point in Mode Two), and concentrating on the sinus system, glissando gently, using full resonance, fairly rapidly to the highest possible pitch. Constantly thinking from a high position, visualise yourself moving through sphenoidal, into ethmoidal, finally into frontal, losing weight and heavier elements, till you are left with the lightest possible timbre resonating in the frontal sinus and nasal bones.

**62ii**  Now reverse the process, returning to your starting note. Repeat a few times, finally remaining on the thin top note comfortably until your breath peters out.

### Lower Mode Two, or pharyngeal register, sometimes erroneously called voice of the throat

To finish this section, we must deal with a vocal area the alternative terms for which can only seem a paradox, given the thesis of the present method. As a general rule, we should remember that 'upper' and 'lower' Mode Two, or 'upper' or 'lower' Mode One refer both to vocal pitches, and a particular tonal quality. They do not describe widely diverse vocal placing, spread anatomically between forehead and lower sternum levels. For, as we have seen, all voice should emanate from a highly-placed system of resonators, *making all voice head voice, in a very real sense*.

But we must admit that, strictly within the context of a convention which assesses the human voice structure in crude, divisive terms like chest and head, the term *voice of the throat* (suggesting, as it does, a vocal capability situated between one mode of production and another, geographically between upper torso and head) has at least some symbolic justification; initially, but *only* initially.

It is essential to underline the importance of this vocal capability to the countertenor. Its range and character are, or should be, the 'meat' of the countertenor voice, and the main instrument for much of its repertoire. Probably, most advanced students, and existing, good countertenors, will have found its exciting tonal strength to be that on which their whole technique seems based, and their voice centred. This is as it should be. Singers wishing to concentrate on the higher, eunuchoid operatic repertoire will, of course, need to encourage this capability upwards in pitch, but always mixed with upper Mode Two. Yet those confusing titles remain, and need comment.

E Herbert Caesari has written expansively and illuminatingly on the pharyngeal register in *The Voice of the Mind*, and this should be studied. Suffice to say here that the hard-toned, 'shelf-like' vocal quality available without forcing is ringing and gratifying to the countertenor singer. It seems almost to act like firm mortar to the bridge region, the *ponticello*, though this image will probably mean something only to he who already possesses the capability. The development and exploitation of it is perhaps best described as being based on a combination of (1) sinus consciousness, and (2) naso-pharynx and soft/hard palate consciousness. The paradoxical term, *voice of the throat*, is thus misleading, and its use liable to lead to problems in the singer's training and technique.

For some people, the image of bouncing the tone on the palate, yet retaining a parallel association with (2), resonance and ease of activity in (1), seems to work for them. Nevertheless, in itself, the phrase *voice of the throat* is the result of the wrong approach to the use of this wonderful and valuable vocal area: a wrong approach which can often allow a fatal tightness to build up in the mouth, throat, and, inevitably (most important of all), the larynx. It is as if the firm mortar has become over-hard, even brittle. The correct approach, however, gives the lie to the offending term *'of the throat'* because the buccal and cranial cavities are always involved. For definite vibrational activity is taking place throughout: in the frontal sinuses, in the ethmoidal cavities, but especially in the sphenoidal sinuses – the nearest of the three-grouped sinus cavities to the pharynx. The maxillary sinuses, and the palate, hard and soft – the partly adjustable roof of the mouth (when open, an additional, adjustable resonating chamber) – are equally involved.

The sheer width and all-embracing quality of tonal activity and the resultant volume, will establish a quasi – but only quasi/upper – Mode One strength, because it will be without the involvement of the vocal folds at their fullest length, as associated with real Mode One. Further study of page 90, in particular column 2, should help the understanding of this.

The treatment of passages like that in exercise 58 is now made clear. High countertenors not wishing to use Mode One capability, or through-voice low countertenors looking to expand the strength of the lower Mode Two tone around the area of transition – the *ponticello* – to upper Mode One, should see, if they have not done so already, the absolute importance of the pharyngeal area.

As would be expected, in all previous sections and exercises we have been concerned generally to develop the lower Mode Two register first, because it is the most important area of the average countertenor's range. When notes have extended in pitch beyond $B_4$, as is suggested on page 91 we have really been using a 'mix' voice quality amalgamating lower Mode Two – and upper Mode Two – areas. We are now ready to consider the upper reaches of Mode Two, used alone.

It must be admitted that the sophisticated development of these, even more than other parts of the countertenor range, are better begun under the careful guidance of a suitable teacher – and hopefully, the present reader may well be him or her; but I present some comment, guidance, suggestions and exercises. Low countertenors of either type are not likely to need overmuch the pipe register to be described, except for very occasional effect. The *tenor altino* type probably will not only eschew its use but also find that he has little potential for it anyway. High countertenors would normally hope to acquire its use for valuable extra range and colour.

We are concerned with two qualities rather than registers: different only through glottal closure variation and a slight shift in resonance:

1. Upper Mode Two – or pure head register.
2. Small register or pipe register.

If the student re-examines the registration diagrams and tables at Figures 5 and 6, he should see that, with the (possible) exception of the modern tenor and the *tenor altino*, plus, perhaps, some heavier 'baritone' Mode One low countertenors; male voices possess an upper thin voice of often potentially very high range. Most female voices possess a corresponding capability at anything more than a fifth or an octave above that of the male. Used alone, these upper vocal qualities can be developed into a pure voice of no great *power* but incredible carrying capability. I mentioned the soprano Calvé in my Preface. Mustapha's teaching enabled her to acquire what she called her 'fourth voice', her small or pipe register. The usual countertenor's fourth voice is, of course, much lower in terms of real pitch, but the acoustic quality resembles the 'soprano pipe' very closely. It can be brilliant and very beautiful, and evokes (even retains?) the quality of the ultra-high boy's voice.

The larynx, unmistakably, is in an extremely raised position for both high head registers, used alone, especially for pipe. Some people might worry about this, but there is no need. An almost constantly high-positioned larynx is perfectly reasonable, for only thus may the particular characteristic tone qualities be achieved; and like the soprano, the countertenor does not usually employ this high extreme for long because it is normally tiring, even produced properly. Some singers, of course, make high work their speciality. For any voice, the upper reaches of Mode Two, used alone, without the addition of lower Mode-Two strength, are not powerful enough to suit big-scale dramatic material. They are best for meditative, delicate works, and brilliant effects in small performing spaces, in very resonant but larger rooms; or for contrasting passages in dramatic works. The student might already be aware of this vocal area, but not perhaps how to use or develop it. Alfred Deller's medium and high notes were excellent examples of it. Of all countertenor vocal areas, these are the most rewarding for *voce bianca* (white voice) effects. *Voce bianca* is, remember, only one of several possible contrasting tonal colours. As can be seen from Figure 5, on page 89, upper Mode Two alone, and pipe register especially, are not so effective below $A_4$ or $G_4$, though they are perfectly tenable there, and this area is useful for beginning their development in the case of some heavier voices. In fact, upper Mode Two quality (not pipe) may be produced down to the start of Mode One, and well beyond, parallel to it; but it is almost useless there except for demonstration of certain therapeutic exercises concerned with the avoidance of a damaging tension, and of the register structure.

### Exercises

The same will be employed for the development of upper Mode Two as for pipe register, because the latter is not so much a change of register as an intensification of the production of the first. But we start with the second, to emphasize the distinctly contrasting sensations to much of what has gone before. First, try the 'wind in the chimney' (exercise 62) again. You should notice that, once past G$\sharp$4 or so, the voice moves automatically into lighter territory. The resonance will be entirely from the frontal sinus and high nasal bones. Repeat for a few minutes, lingering longer at the higher pitch to make the voice ready for the next stage. Only when it feels well warmed in the higher reaches, consider moving on.

**63i** Say KAH very gently, first in upper Mode Two, as in normal speech, then again without producing any tone at all, preserving only the KAH movement at the base of the tongue. Observe in a looking glass the effect of the K alone on the position of the larynx: it raises it considerably. Extend it as KAH, and the larynx sinks again. As explained hitherto, pipe register is usually done with permanently raised larynx, as if the K restriction thins the airwave out towards resonance high above. You must visualise the frontal sinuses, aiming *almost behind and certainly above them*, and very high indeed; as if away and out of the skull, like a small halo. At the same time, say KAH again; this time in medium highish Mode Two, above G4; then hum the same note. Soon, it will be noticed that the hum has modified itself in the KAH, has shifted slightly, acquiring a new, extra clear *unearthly* dimension. Tilt the head perhaps half a degree *downwards*, if this helps to establish this modified placing, then sing exercise ii, at A4, A$\sharp$4 or B4, whichever feels most comfortable. Repeat a few times, never allowing weighty tone to intrude, however soft in volume. Work to refine and lighten. Think thin and forward-high, searching for that one point of optimum purity, *pianissimo* in volume. Do not employ a tight, explosive K in any way – rather use a K with a G mixed in it. Sound it with an easy tongue action.

**63ii**

Return at intervals to this over a period of days, till this new, differing timbre feels established. Some people may need longer.

**63iii**  Now try the other vowels, Italian and English, each preceded by K, all on the same B4. Aim at a clear, thin, piccolo-like timbre as you ascend. This is easier in some vowels than in others. Do not distort any. AH, OO, o (hot), AW, OH (mow), U and I (high), are the best to start with: e (egg), EE, AY, a (er) are left till later. *Do not practise this work for long: it can be tiring; but do not move to iv until i–iii are mastered.*

**63iv**

Keep the mouth still. All movement is in the tongue root (and therefore the larynx, because they are connected). Touch the short notes lightly, almost *staccato*. Treat each bar as a separate exercise. Then alternate the seven sounds within the phrase. If found too high to sustain initially, begin a tone down, on G#4.

**63v**

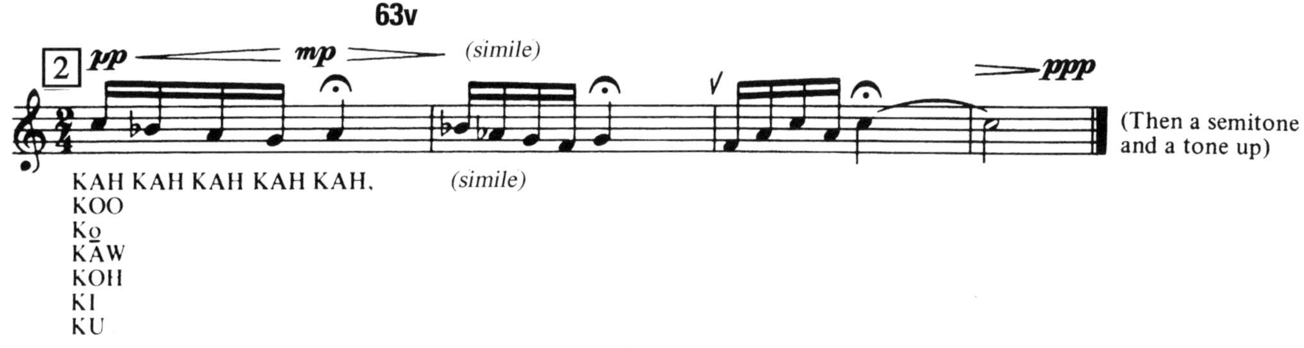

Again, use only the seven vowels above. Gradually make these modest extremes of volume more marked. The highest notes should be thin, brilliant, with a harmonic edge to them. Do not allow the *crescendos* to bloom too much, to become too full in tone. Retain the 'high above skull, above frontal sinus' image. This exercise is fatiguing: again, do not work at it for long. Imagine a *fining* of each note and sound, pure and sharp-toned as a needlepoint.

**63vi**   The more difficult sounds may best be formed via the easier ones. Try to retain brilliance in the four higher-tongued vowels. Pinch the tone *slightly*, but do not distort or force. Remember that these remaining vowels can never be as sparkling as the first seven, but are capable of borrowing some of their quality, with practice.

Most students should by now have acquired some facility in the small or pipe register. Pipe *quality* should be evident in the tone. It is possible, however, that some heavier voices, and *tenors altino*, have not managed to establish this effect: not everybody has effective access to it. Re-examine Figure 5, page 89. All countertenors would expect to use the less precious, yet light, upper Mode Two, a quality perhaps best visualised and experienced as half lower Mode Two, half small register, and already familiar at the top of the 'wind in the chimney'. Concentrate only on the frontal sinus and nasal bones. Repeat the 'wind in the chimney' exercise now. This brings upper Mode Two quality back into notes which have recently been sung in pipe register. Do not allow any heavier, firmer sensation to creep in. The next exercise (64) is designed for use in both (i) upper Mode Two, and (ii) small registers, *separately*, in that order. Consciously use these slightly contrasting versions of the notes available at the top of your voice. Try the exercise in F major if desired, but monitor the two qualities carefully.

**64**

It is almost impossible to describe the differences between these registers verbally. Remember that small or pipe arises directly from the development of upper Mode Two, is an ultra-thin version of it: is almost as much sensation as sound or timbre, when assessed from within. Watch for a tendency to sing sharp as the pitch ascends.

At the next exercise, use the pitch given and the dynamics as shown. Sing it slowly to start with, stopping to correct vowels as necessary. Decide which vocal option to employ as you reach the halfway area of the ascending scale: upper Mode Two or pipe register.

Speed up only when intonation and vocal placing are secure and even in timbre:

**65**

i.  *(All vowel sounds, starting with AH, throughout.)*
ii.  I will sing my halftones ev'-ry day till they are per – fect.    I will sing my halftones ev'ry day till they are per-fect.

Then try the exercise in various higher pitches. It is useful for checking intonation lower in the voice. Through-voice countertenors should work

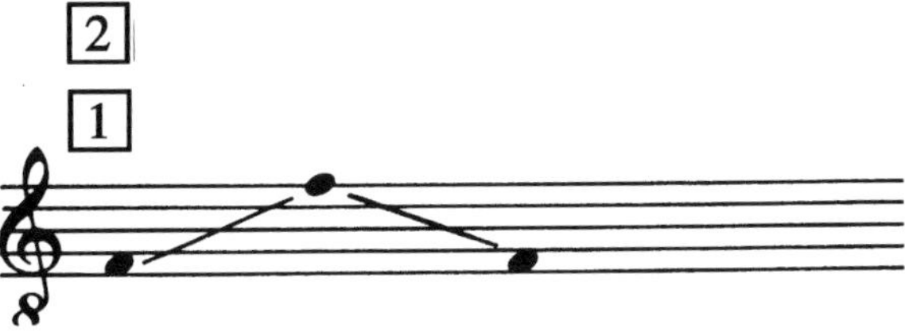

at about:
when using the exercise for general practice.

**66**    Now return to exercises 43 and 55 (pages 66 and 75), and indeed any previous exercises that appear useful for upper Mode Two or pipe reg-

**67**

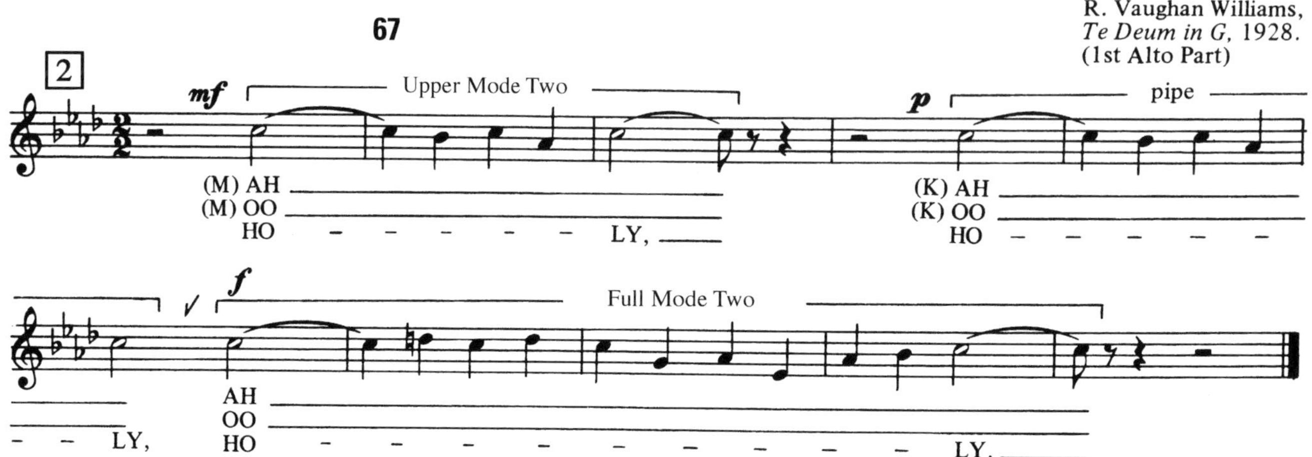



ister practice. In particular, try exercise 63 i–vi to test your ability to use either option at the same pitch, using the same vowels.

Use the above exercise to alternate upper Mode Two with pipe and full Mode Two mix, as indicated. (The latter is the re-assembling of the full voice after using its different elements separately.) Then interchange the three passages, using different qualities and different vowels. Repeat a few times only.

**68i, ii**

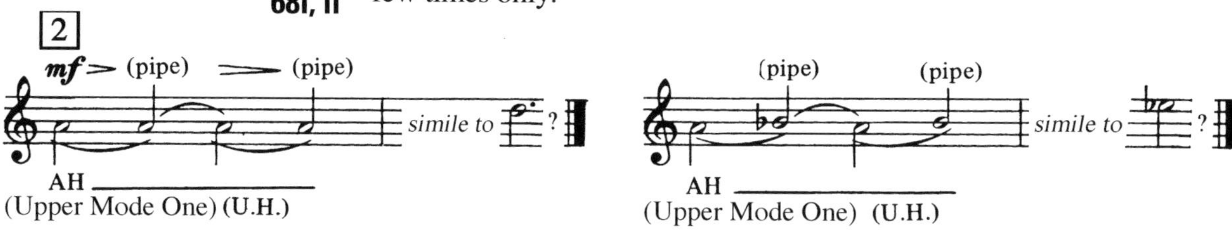



These exercises further help to perfect smoother interplay of the two separate high-area qualities available as alternative timbres. At first, use M to initiate the note, inserting K to help the change to pipe quality, then M and K to finish. Do not work these for long, or attempt high notes too soon. Always aim at comfort and vocal ease. Eliminate both M and K as soon as possible. Use the dynamics as indicated in 69i.

**69**

**68iii**   *Simile,* using the interval of a tone.

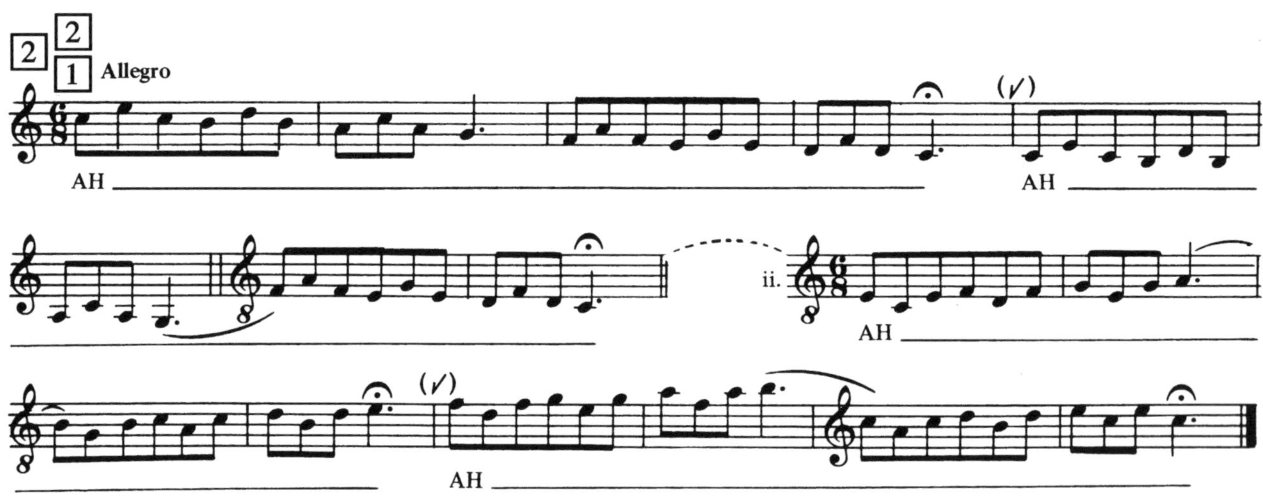
Allegro
AH
AH
ii.
AH
AH

**69**  In the excerpt on page 105 (from *Ode for Queen Anne's Birthday*, 1713, by Handel), various upper Mode Two, small register, plus full Mode-Two mix effects, may have been expected or hoped-for by the composer. The normal 18th century use of the alto clef has caused the part to appear even higher than it is, thus perhaps suggesting a tonal quality or

**70ii**  qualities. The thin, carrying timbre of the resultant vocal tone would

sound well with that of a hautboy. The student is advised to try the exercise first as a series of separate passages, linking them finally only when each is mastered. Add the words when vocal technique and music are convincingly settled together. The excerpt may be sung down a semitone, because this could more nearly approximate the pitch of the Handel period. Because this particular aria is clearly for high countertenor, lower voices may wish to omit it, or sing selected passages only. All countertenors are advised to peruse a copy of the whole work, in which may be found excellent material for study, because Handel used two solo countertenors, one of high type, one of low.

**70i**  Two final, all-embracing exercises for agility, range, even tone and sinus resonation balance. Use all vowels, beginning with AH.
Exercise 70i is suitable for all countertenors if started and finished at a comfortable point. It could be transposed or extended for very high

voices. Work to eliminate the breath point as soon as possible. Indeed, many students will find no need for it at all. Then try to extend your breath control towards combining both parts of the exercise to form a single eloquent demonstration of the range, control and quality of your vocal instrument.

Also convert the above exercise to the greater scale, retaining the same time signature.

Russell Oberlin is a *tenor altino*, but his cadenza is suitable for most countertenor types.

**71**    *A good method of practising breath control and development.*
Remove any restrictive clothing round the waist. Lie on your back, placing one hand on the abdomen and the other on the lower ribs. Inhale through the nose, slowly, deeply, evenly, without jerking or interruption. If this is done properly, the abdomen will gradually increase in size without trembling, the lower ribs expanding sideways, while the upper chest and collarbones remain undisturbed. Now hold your breath, not by shutting the glottis (the aperture through the vocal folds) or shutting the nasal passages, but by keeping the midriff down and the chest walls extended. Count four mentally at the speed of one per second, and then let the breath go suddenly. This results in the flying up of the midriff and a falling of the ribs: a collapse of the lower body. The contrasts will become apparent with repeated practice. Do not hold your breath to begin with for more than four seconds and do not tire yourself out with this exercise. Repeat at intervals. Breathing capacity will increase. Eventually, you will be able to breath abdominally whilst standing. Make certain you retain the same physical sensations as when lying down. Gradually increase the time of holding the breath.

Now reverse things: rapid inspiration and slow expiration: even, jerk-less, uninterrupted, smooth.

(Based on Behnke, *The Mechanism of the Human Voice*, 19th Ed. 1888, pp. 106–8.)

# Some final thoughts

As this basic course nears its close, the student is advised to regard it merely as a beginning. His vocal instrument should now be effective in all parts of its range, and control should be considerable. Next come consolidation, further study, and always more practice, using these and other exercises. With all this comes use of the instrument for its appropriate repertoire. But a few reflections are in order.

Though it had never faded totally from the scene, the countertenor, or alto, as a recognised solo voice, was in effect re-established by Deller, then Whitworth and Oberlin, in the 1940s and early 1950s. It was not an easy path. We now live in days of comparative plenty and expertise in male high singing. But idiosyncrasy, human nature and fashion being what they are, there seems to be something of a reaction. Despite excellent, high-profile countertenors like Andreas Scholl and David Daniels stunning listeners with their artistry and skill, much of the repertoire they and other superb countertenors sing today was intended for castrati, or general use (and there can be no objection to this). Unfortunately, less use is being made of the countertenor voice family for its original repertoire, both solo and in ensemble. Why? Though, no doubt, musicological experiment is partly responsible, avoidance of the use of the high male voice in music written with the implicit expectation of this vocal type (in works clearly intended for it in context, style, and historical date) often seems contrived. Such practice is based, apparently, on considerations, even perhaps preoccupations, not always genuinely concerned with authentic musical and historical procedure.

As I suggested at the outset, it is probably inevitable in a course of this kind, that some teachers and singers may decide that certain aspects are over-expanded, over-contracted, or even missing. However, it is the hope of the author that the course achieves a reasonable balance, and that it might go some way towards providing teachers and would-be countertenors with a basic reference and handbook with which to start or continue study of this marvellous vocal genre.

We might end with the thought that because music, as with any other art form, reflects the age in which it is composed and performed, it is not surprising that *countertenors vary and have varied in order to meet the demands of the age in which they serve*. Always excepting the later Romantic period, when he was heard almost only in church music and glees, and with limited tonal variety, the countertenor seems variously to have been ringing, nasal, clear, piercing and strong: some or most of these qualities would always have been readily available. Yet his palette of colours also included the delicate, the round, the subtle, and the languishing. The student is urged to investigate the possibilities of his own voice-type and range: not only for the authentic performance of major and less major music of the past, but also works of today already composed, and those yet to be born.

Surely here is a particularly singular instrument. All voices sing a single line, but the sound of the male high-voice is *ultra-linear* – if not always thin, then essentially lithe. It is decidedly otherworldly, inhabiting a strange, unreal macrocosm somewhere inside the head; indefinable, but so obviously more than falsetto.

A PERSONAL POSTSCRIPT
*My years of performing, of practical and theoretical research, of thinking hard and listening widely, have perhaps encouraged me to become something of a walking vocal test-bed. It is for the student to use and benefit from this, and from my five-decades' love affair with the haunting quality of the countertenor or alto voice.*

# Booklist for further practical work and study

The list below is emphatically not an exhaustive and exclusive academic bibliography, but is quite simply a small, recommended collection of useful works, chosen judiciously. Many others demanded inclusion, but I had to resist them for reasons both of space and focus. (My magnum opus, *The History and Technique of the Counter-Tenor*, listed below, will yield more titles for those desirous of further reading.) Some in the present list are useful only in part, care being needed not to be influenced by any material contradictory in content to the present method and its basis. I have indicated something of the strengths of each work and its particular use to the teacher and counter-tenor student. It is, of course, impossible to confirm that all are in print at present, but all should be obtainable through a public or other library. In London, Westminster Music Library, in Victoria, is recommended.

I emphasise that the purpose of the present work is to help the student to sing, not primarily to research. The following are listed on this basis. Asterisked titles are particularly useful for a teacher.


*BEHNKE, EMIL *The Mechanism of the Human Voice*. Curwen, 1888.
A very important manual by a leading 19th-century authority. Excellent basic information from an (enlightened) mechanistic point of view.

BEHNKE, KATE EMIL *The Technique of Singing*. Williams and Norgate, 1945.
An excellent general handbook (by Behnke's daughter) if one ignores the authoress's views on 'falsetto', which are neither ours nor indeed her father's. Therefore, for *falsetto* read *collapsed falsetto*, and all will be well.

*BUTENSCHØN & BORCHGREVINK *Voice and Song*. Cambridge Univ. Press, 1982.
Though somewhat inhibiting, and in places fundamentally different in view from the present work, it is useful anatomically, and a fascinating thesis.

*CAESARI E. HERBERT *The Voice of the Mind*. Robert Hale Ltd, 1963 (2nd Edition).
Excellent, though very involved and not always quite in line with the present work. Especially useful for the chapter on the pharyngeal register, which is very much in line with it!

CLEALL, CHARLES *Voice Production in Choral Technique*. Novello (1970 Edition).
A valuable book for singers of all voice types, solo or choral, which includes much varied matter on general vocal education.

*COFFIN, BERTON *Overtones of Bel Canto*. Scarecrow Press, N.Y. 1980.
An extremely detailed original thesis, very useful to the countertenor.

DONINGTON, ROBERT *The Interpretation of Early Music*. Faber and Faber (1975 Edition).
This huge classic should be in the possession of anyone involved in early music, though even Donington seems unclear on certain aspects of the countertenor/alto question.

*DUMVILLE, BENJAMIN *The Science of Speech*. University Tutorial Press, London, (2nd Edition 1926).
Despite the coincidentally unapt surname of its author, this important work, subtitled *An Elementary Manual of English Phonetics for Teachers*, is useful; especially for Americans and others who might find it difficult to relate the sung vowels given in the present work to their own everyday pronunciation.

FRISELL, ANTHONY *The Tenor Voice*. Bruce Humphries, Boston, 1964.
An excellent handbook of use and real interest to the countertenor.

FRISELL, ANTHONY *The Baritone Voice*. Crescendo Publishing Co. Boston. 1973
See above.

GARCIA, MANUEL *The Art of Singing*. Darewski, London, 1847 Edition; Boston, Ditson, 1855.
A very important work by the most influential 19th-century authority. Of great interest to the countertenor, though Garcia's terminology needs to be taken with qualification.

GARDINER, JULIAN *A Guide to Good Singing and Speech*. Cassell, 1968.
A fine handbook, but be warned – the author does not much like countertenors! Especially useful for English and Italian vowel formation, breathing and registers (though not seen from the countertenor's viewpoint).

*GILES, PETER *The History and Technique of the Counter-Tenor*. Scolar Press, Ashgate, 1994.
This truly magnum opus, which totally replaces Giles's *The Counter-Tenor* (Muller) as the only truly comprehensive work on the subject, is essential as a companion volume to the present Method.

*GILES, PETER *Les Contreténors: Mythes & Réalités*. Harmonia Mundi, HMB 590017.18,1999.
A unique work: part concise version of the above work, part recorded anthology of 17 contrasted countertenors on two CDs; all tracks selected by the author to illustrate his thesis. An essential companion to this Method.

*GREENE, MARGARET *The Voice and its Disorders*. Pitman (Reprint 1972).
This, the speech therapist's handbook, is an excellent work for singers too. Though the authoress is rather cool on the subject of the countertenor, and indeed misunderstands sinus-control method, the work is strongly recommended.

*HEWLETT, ARTHUR *Think Afresh About the Voice*. E G White Society, Thames Publishing, 1987.
A fascinating extension and very slight qualification of the ideas of E G White, and his School of Sinus Tone Production. Unorthodox but stimulating, and invaluable to the countertenor.

* KENNEDY SCOTT, CHARLES *The Fundamentals of Singing*. Cassell, 1954.
A modern classic comprehensive handbook, rich in explanation. Though it does not deal specifically with the countertenor, it is an essential reference and practical work.

LEHMANN, LILLI *How to Sing*. Macmillan, New York, 1914.
An invaluable handbook by an eminent singer trained in the *bel canto* tradition. Though there is nothing specifically about the high male voice, this practical work is a thoughtful insight into the personal approach of an artist who worked through a particularly interesting vocal epoch.

*MILLER, RICHARD *The English, French, German and Italian Techniques of Singing*. The Scarecrow Press, Metuchen, N.J., 1977.
I recommend this book with quite some hesitation, for I cannot possibly support all the views, arguments, and conclusions therein, especially inrelation to falsetto, head voice, and the countertenor. (Miller rejects totally any artistic use of falsetto, both in the past and today.) But I feel that despite this the work is important and useful. It sets out in fine detail the differing ways in which the four main schools of singing approach vocal pedagogy. Thus, there is much of great value in this book; but be warned: after digesting its massive information, take care note to suffer inhibition. It could be said that in this study lies danger for the practising singer, who could find himself unconsciously or indeed consciously trying to adopt more than one technique at a time. But I still recommend it because it offers glimpses to techniques used by the male voices of four different countries in the past, inasmuch as no national tendencies or technique could have left any voice type or range untouched and uninfluenced.

PUNT, NORMAN A *The Singer's and Actor's Throat*. Heinemann Medical, 1952. (Third Revision, 1974).
A small bible on voice-care, and matters relating.

REID, CORNELIUS *The Free Voice*. Joseph Patelson, Music House, 1965. (Reprint 1974).
A comprehensive and excellent manual, in the main.

VACCAI, NICCOLO *Practical Italian Vocal Method*. Kalmus, New York (for Alto or Baritone); Peters Edition 1914 reprinted (for high voice).
An invaluable and important work, which offers *not* voice production but a step-by-step singers' musicianship course. It combines well with most methods of teaching voice production. It is strongly recommended as a companion to the present work. Vaccai was born in 1790 and died in 1848, which places his famous treatise at the end of the prime period of Italian *bel canto* singing. The countertenor is recommended to acquire both editions for the reasons given on page 77.

*WHITE, ERNEST *Science and Singing*. Dent 1938 (Reprinted 1950).
The original work on sinus tone production must be recommended for its illuminating thesis and detailed examination of the cranial cavities. It is an historic work; a reaction to the almost total emphasis in singing pedagogy of the larynx and its workings by the early 20th century. The original book dates from 1909, and went through several editions (one under the title *The Voice Beautiful*), but the recommended one is that of 1938.